Expanded Praise for *Midsize*

"*Midsize* is just what our hundreds of companies needed to unlock growth! Each of our presidents is optimizing their marketing based on Julia's story-based teachings and practical guidance."

—Larry Gies, Founder & CEO Madison Industries

"Fitzgerald pairs her Kellogg MBA with real-life experiences to share marketing wisdom that works. She delivers a smart, pragmatic guide for driving growth in midsize companies in any business sector. For professionals seeking purpose and satisfaction from their work, *Midsize* illustrates that size matters."

—Harry Kraemer, Former Chairman and CEO of Baxter International and Professor at Northwestern University Kellogg School of Management

"Want to get your company from $100 million to over $1 billion in sales? Read this book—and keep a notepad handy. *Midsize* is a wonderful read: rich with personal stories and hard-earned insights that anyone working at a midsize company could put to good use right away."

—Drew Neisser, Founder Renegade + CMO Huddles, author of *Renegade Marketing: 12 Steps to Building Unbeatable B2B Brands*

"I've been CEO at a ten-person start-up and CMO at a public company. One thing is certain—good marketing can take any size company from good to great and a good marketing job can take a junior executive to the top of any organization. *Midsize* is a must read for anyone thinking about what's next."

—Nancy MacIntyre, General Manager and CMO Game Taco, former CEO and Co-Founder Fingerprint, Former CMO LeapFrog

"The actionable takeaways in *Midsize* are a great guide for any CMO looking to make a big impact with limited resources. You will laugh at the anecdotes and stories, but this playbook offers some serious wisdom and advice."

—Amy Pzywara, CMO, Sylvan Learning

"This book is a must read for marketers with a general management and growth mindset. Midsize delivers insights and strategies that are clearly rooted in experience and delivered with both wit and wisdom."

—Karen Kaplan, Chair & CEO, Hill Holliday

"Post-pandemic, we find ourselves in the middle of the "great resignation." Employees want an organization where they can grow and thrive. *Midsize* is their answer: this book will help them determine what type of company can match their drive and disposition."

—Sarah Krikorian, CHRO, American Lung Association

MIDSIZE

MIDSIZE

The Truths and Strategies of Marketing in Midsize Firms

JULIA FITZGERALD

Published By:
Redwood Publishing, LLC
Orange County, California
www.redwooddigitalpublishing.com

Printed in the United States of America

ISBN 978-1-956470-59-8 (hardcover)
ISBN 978-1-956470-60-4 (paperback)
ISBN 978-1-956470-61-1 (ebook)
Library of Congress Control Number: 2022917050

Cover Design: Michelle Manley
Interior Design: Jose Pepito
Copyediting and Proofreading: Avery Auer

TABLE OF CONTENTS

FINDING YOUR FIT AND MAKING IT WORK

recently attended a reunion at my beloved business school. One of the great features of these events is that it blends alumni from a range of graduating classes with the freshly minted grads. At one of the mixers, I asked a group of new marketing-focused graduates where they had taken positions. One replied, "Revlon," one was going to a licensing firm, and another was still looking for the right fit. I asked if they'd found their positions through the school's placement services and on-campus recruiting. All three of these students answered, "No." The companies that recruited on campus were big brands within their fields and large organizations. Each of these marketers was looking for something different. They wanted a situation where they could use the breadth of the management degree they'd earned—not just their marketing expertise. This sounded very familiar to me; it was a similar situation when I graduated over twenty years ago.

That's when I had an aha moment. Top business schools tend to teach marketing courses to make the students successful at the large corporations that recruit on campus and support the school. Large corporations continue to recruit at these schools because the curriculum prepares students to be successful in their environments. This is a bit of an oversimplification, as almost all business schools also have tracks that prepare students for marketing and general management at start-ups and other entrepreneurial ventures. But there is a definite gap for students, such as the three new alumni eating cocktail snacks and drinking wine with me. Who prepares the grad students for marketing at midsize companies? After all, these companies account for a large percentage of employers worldwide.

I have spent my career in the field of marketing. For me, it has always been the perfect blend of creativity and delivering measurable results. I tell people that I get the same satisfaction from a good marketing plan as I do from working a jigsaw puzzle. Coming out of undergrad, I had the opportunity to work at a couple of midsize companies in Los Angeles prior to heading to business school. So my sense of how business was run was built around smaller, scrappy organizations versus well-resourced, larger corporations. I was fortunate to have some great mentors early on who showed me the importance of having a marketing team that was well synched with the sales, inventory, customer service, and HR teams. One of my goals related to this book is to connect with people seeking to succeed in marketing at a midsize company and share some of the strategies that have worked in multiple business models and changing business environments.

WHY NOW?

In light of COVID and the Great Resignation, there has been a huge turnover of people who decided they were unhappy with their place in the workforce. They want to spend their days feeling productive, balanced, and engaged. So finding a good match is more important than ever. There seems to be a national permission to reassess and let yourself work where you're going to have a fulfilling experience. Marketing people tend to be a blend of creative and analytical talents, and they really deserve to find the right fit for their skills and preferences. It's a good moment in time to consider the size of the organization you choose and how that impacts your day-to-day engagement and happiness. Find your jam.

I'm one of the lucky few who's had a chance to work at both large and midsize organizations and at multiple companies in various industries. I bring more than twenty years of experience in corporate life, as well as insight and anecdotes from other colleagues and professionals in the space. My unique work history allows me to tell this story and hopefully help others draw conclusions about where they may fit.

WHO CARES?

Maybe nobody; time will tell. But these insights may be especially valuable for you if you fall into one of these three categories:

1. Early career marketers or students asking, "How do I think about marketing?" and "What might be right for me?"

This is the marketing student who is choosing their career path, or even a person early in their career who might be in one situation but is contemplating a move. Since these readers are the next generation, in this book I'll call them **Next Gen** for short.

2. CEOs making savvy decisions about their marketing department.

This is the CEO or leadership in a growth-mode company who's looking at their marketing department and trying to figure out how to staff it or what to prioritize for success. In many cases, the CEO is not a marketing person; they frequently come from finance or operations. Now they're trying to right-size/be savvy about their marketing investment. CEOs stepping into a private equity portfolio company leadership role may also find this useful.

3. CMOs who are potentially organization changers or new to a midsize company.

This is the CMO who is wondering, for example, "What would a marketing department look like if I took the plunge and left Amazon and went to work for the American Lung Association or Portillo's?" According to the research consultancy Gartner, the average tenure of a CMO is approximately twenty-six months, so it stands to reason that a CMO may find some helpful perspective in choosing their own paths or building strong practices in a midsize company.

DOES SIZE REALLY MATTER?

From strategy and organization to agency support and budgeting, working in a midsize company has a unique set of challenges and rewards. For clarity, by "midsize" firms I am referring to companies with revenues greater than $100 million and less than $1 billion. These are frequently growth-phase companies and may be PE-owned firms. As a midsize firm, they have outgrown the exciting start-up phase in which raising funds and driving initial success are the primary goals. At $100 million-plus, a firm now needs staff and discipline that can help it profitably scale from a start-up or find new growth levers if the company has plans to grow to the coveted $1 billion-plus level.

Firms with revenues in this range generally are not prepared to take on an outsized payroll commitment to drive future business. Most growth-phase companies would prefer to generate the demand and revenue and then commit to the resources along the growth curve. As a marketer, you will need to be scrappy, efficient, and able to pull off big changes without big internal teams for support. It's a different set of skills than what is needed in large firms where staff can specialize, wear one distinct hat, and have clean interdepartmental handoffs. More than likely, the successful marketing staffer in a midsize company will have functional specialties *and* the ability to collaborate and reach across multiple disciplines.

After working at a couple of multibillion-dollar companies and leading marketing departments in several B2C and B2B midsize companies, I have boiled down the experiences to a few key areas in which there are different realities and where size *does* matter:

1. **Budgets:** In general, they are smaller (*scrappy, stewardship, & ROI* are the watchwords).

2. **Strategy:** There is no separate strategy department or project management department.

3. **Collaboration:** Cross-functional coordination is key for success.

4. **Digital Marketing:** This gives midsize companies a real chance to compete with goliaths.

5. **Innovation and Critical Thinking:** People who love what they do tend to thrive at midsize companies. Ideas and problem-solving can and must come from all individuals. Showing up really matters.

I'm not here to hard-sell a career path at a midsize company but rather to point out some key considerations when you are looking to choose an employer or perhaps staff your team. Also, every company has its own DNA, so these observations will not hold true in every case.

The appeal of a larger or smaller company may change for the marketer depending on life stage, other interests in life, or changes in the marketplace. I left a rewarding position at a midsize toy company because digital marketing and e-commerce was exploding. I knew if I wanted to stay relevant in marketing and excel in the digital arena, I needed to go somewhere where they could afford to be on the digital cutting edge and where they have a buttload of data to get the most out of evolving analytics tools. That's right; I'm talking about retail! I joined a multibillion-dollar retailer where I could learn the power of digital marketing and transformation at scale. It was an experience I would never get at my former midsize employer. They simply did not have the budgets or reach to maximize digital advertising, e-commerce, analytics, social, etc.

Large-Company Benefits	Large-Company Drawbacks
Resume building and brand recognition	Potentially less flexibility for individuals
Resources and bigger marketing budgets	More tightly scripted positions
Room to grow and advance career	Competition for leadership positions tougher, with more employees
Training programs	Longer time to implement new ideas, changes
Short- and long-term compensation options, generally strong benefits packages	A lot of time and focus spent on internal budgeting and reporting
Network of colleagues	More time spent on internal coordination, potentially taking focus from the customer and the competitive environment
Strategic frameworks	Marketing team may feel removed from the strategic planning
Specialized departments can excel in specific areas (analytics, customer service, materials development, communications)	Harder to have flow of cross-functional ideas and collaboration

In one of my post-undergrad early positions, I had a great VP of marketing, Norb G., who told me, "Oh, Julia, you're doing it all backward. What you should have done is gone to a big conglomerate to begin with. Then you would have those brands on your resume, and you would understand that they suck out your soul, and then you would go to graduate school and go to some smaller, cool place. And you would eventually become their CMO. I think you got this reversed." Of course, I was thinking, "Norb, I have no idea what you're talking about." But years later, I get what Norb was trying to tell me. And I'm sharing it now because I want you to ask this question of yourselves: **What is the right fit?**

In Part One of this book, we'll talk about the makings of a midsize. I'll share various truths from my experience and that of others, including the distinctive qualities, challenges, and opportunities of marketing for midsize companies. We'll discuss managing the narrative, team organization, cross-company collaboration, branding, and knowing your customer.

In Part Two, we'll move into tangible strategies and secrets for success. We'll look at making digital ecosystems, content marketing, digital advertising, social media, and KPIs work for the midsize organization.

For anyone taking on a marketing role or a general management role at a midsize company, I hope you will find some useful insights in these chapters. After a career of building businesses at both midsize and large companies, I'm ready to share the truths, secrets, and strategies for success.

PART
ONE

THE MAKINGS
OF A MIDSIZE

CHAPTER ONE

MANAGING THE NARRATIVE:

"WE'RE A LIFESTYLE BRAND"

When you work at a large company, odds are that people know what the enterprise does. Your firm may not be a household name like Amazon, General Motors, or United Airlines, but if you are bigger than $1 billion in revenue, your customers and potential customers probably know what you do. If you are a smaller organization, you need to make the answer to this question clear: **What is it you do and for whom?**

It sounds so simple, you'd think I wouldn't have to write about this. Yet here I am, typing the truth as the first marketing challenge to tackle.

I'll give you an example. Recently, in a moment of weakness, I picked up my ringing office phone for an unanticipated call. Of course, it was a sales pitch, and the person told me he could help me grow my business if I would just take twenty minutes to describe my marketing model. Intrigued by the absurdity of the request, I asked what his company did. He began a rambling description of work in digital channels that connects platforms with media and paid digital that uses proprietary technology to improve how blah, blah, blah. I politely ended the call without remembering the company's name or what the heck they did.

The telesales person can't be blamed for a bad script. The marketing team should have worked out the narrative. Who is the company? And what problem do they solve and for whom? It takes some time to really sharpen the language that describes the value proposition. There may be an internal bias to throw in everything the company does, which is not the same as its value proposition.

When working with the American Lung Association, a quintessential midsize organization, we found that despite strong name recognition, people did not know what the company does. The first impulse from the staff was to laundry-list all the different ALA activities. Smoking cessation, clean air advocacy, lung cancer support, asthma training, walks and climbs, a clinical trial network, and on and on. But that did not help the average person understand what the Lung Association actually *does*. They advocate, educate, and provide research funds for public lung health. They are the trusted champions of lung health for the American public. Period. Full stop. All of the other details can be found in ads, on websites, on social media platforms, etc.

A company's narrative is at its very core. It's almost personal, and all marketing and communications need to be built on it.

The ideal communication scenario is one in which the company name or the primary brand helps tell the story. This is especially helpful for a midsize company, as it saves time and money in awareness building. Has there ever been a better company name than Toys "R" Us? No mystery around what they do. If that complete clarity is not possible, taglines, elevator pitches, and digital copy all need to nail the narrative.

In my early career, I worked for a company called P. Leiner. It was a great company with an awful name. While I think it was named after a founder, it just made me think of "panty liners." But that was *not* the product. P. Leiner sold private-label vitamins and OTCs (over-the-counter drugs) to drug and grocery retailers across the country. They were the largest private-label manufacturer, and they met FDA standards and maintained impeccable quality standards. Back in those days, P. Leiner—which has since changed its name and been acquired—earned annual revenues between $200 million and $300 million. The management team knew the value proposition was to get a quality private-label product to retailers that would allow them to make higher profit margins with their own house brand. That message was on all of our B2B messaging, even though the company name did not help tell our story. The company also provided customer service and customized promotional plans to retailers, but that clearly was not critical to our value prop. We all knew that quality product with a private-label brand and a value price was our narrative.

Fast-forward to business school after leaving P. Leiner. I had a job interview with one of the large branded OTC drug companies. Halfway through the interview, it became clear that the company interviewer agreed to put me on his roster only because he wanted details about the P. Leiner business model. He finally asked, "Didn't you feel bad about working for a company that just drains the margin out of a whole product category?" At this point, it was safe to assume that there was no intent to offer me a position, so I asked him about his company's value prop: "Do *you* ever feel bad about overcharging for a product that could make people feel better? Because we both know how little it costs to manufacture those tablets. Of the two of us, I don't think I am the one who should feel bad!" And I picked up my bag and walked out.

I was correct: no job offer. His company's narrative was about a brand you would trust with your health. P. Leiner was about good product at a value. Both companies did an excellent job living their narratives, and there was room in the market for both.

AN OLD-SCHOOL CONCEPT

The elevator pitch. It's an old concept. And since COVID-19, hardly anyone gets in an elevator with a stranger—but humor me. Can you tell people what your company does and for whom in the span of a couple of floors? Would everyone in the organization say the same thing? The messaging starts with internal staff and moves out in concentric rings from there. If this sounds familiar, like your Marketing 101 class on positioning, *bingo!* It is the same basic principle that so often gets overlooked. What does your company do and for whom? What problem does it solve?

Why do I bring this up for the midsize company? My experience is that within a large organization, this work is usually already done. Or there may be an assigned corporate communications team that hammers out this kind of messaging. But in a smaller firm that may be in growth mode, the marketing team needs to get this messaging nailed so all communications build on it.

If there is no internal agreement on the company's narrative and value proposition, this is a red flag. I have seen companies without a clear value prop stay afloat for years, delivering one-off whatevers until customers move on for better price, brand, or product innovation. An unfortunate example of this is a company that was a household product and name decades ago. Despite a long heritage, the company lost its narrative. It had stopped investing in its brand, its product was no longer innovative or patent protected, and its cost of goods was still high. It could not position itself as a clear "best brand story," and other OEM manufacturers produced similar products at lower prices. So they did not have a better value or margin positioning. When this manufacturer went to pitch retailers during the seasonal product reviews, they did not have a compelling story of how they fit into the offerings for the retailers' shoppers. Year after year, the company's presence on retailers' shelves—both brick-and-mortar and online—shrank. Meanwhile, some competitors in the space took the preferred brand positioning, and others claimed the private label or value positioning.

Lost in the middle without a clear value proposition is a bad place to be. However, an organization that knows its value will also know how to evolve with changing environments and find customers who will benefit from its business model.

Kim Feil, the Chief Marketing & Strategy Officer of Aspire Brands, has enjoyed a long and storied career. She has run the full gamut as a CMO—from commanding a billion-dollar marketing budget at Walgreens and multimillion-dollar budgets at Sara Lee and OfficeMax to growing midsize and startup companies. "Believe me," she told me, "the big brands can be exhilarating. With big budgets you can fund big, bold ideas. But the effort of bringing a big idea to life in a large organization can also be daunting."

When Kim was at IRI, a global data analytics and research company, she worked with a lot of midsize accounts. "The best of them had one thing in common," she said. "They had an exceptionally clear vision and value proposition. One that comes to mind is B&G Foods. At the time, they had a few solid but smaller brands and were best known for their pickle and relish products. Their value proposition was to deliver these 'center aisle' brands to grocers with high-impact packaging, service, and branded promotions to become a preferred vendor in consumer staples. B&G was midsize when I first encountered them, but their strategy drove their acquisition plans, and they continue to grow their business to this day. They have acquired over twenty brands and have moved far beyond the midsize category by executing their value proposition strategy."

These days, Kim has moved away from research consulting and into the realm of healthy energy drinks. She discovered the ASPIRE Healthy Energy Drinks when she was serving on the board of a Wisconsin-based retailer, Roundy's. She eventually became a board member and advisor to Aspire. She was extremely impressed with the product—a healthy energy drink that had a clear value proposition: no calories or sugar, vegan, kosher, with the right amount of natural caffeine and vitamins for smooth, sustained energy—and it tastes great. Aspire is a drink for people who aspire to do more and live a healthy lifestyle. Kim has a keen interest in products that are natural and help people live healthier lives, so it was a perfect fit.

At the behest of the co-founders, she eventually joined the staff as CMO and CSO, where she has shared their journey into the midsize territory. When she started, their sales had just topped $250,000; now, they have distribution in major retailers around the country and online. The week I talked with Kim, she squeezed me in between their launch at Costco's Midwest stores and their sampling programs throughout the Chicagoland area.

"There are so many things I appreciate about being at a midsize, like Aspire," she said. "I love being deeply invested in the team. As we bring on more junior members, I love to coach them and bring them along as they develop. I like contributing my skill and knowledge about strategy, fundraising, and marketing to the founders' and co-CEOs' complementary expertise. We make do with a lean staff as long as possible, and as we double and triple in size, we scale the team. It's satisfying to build out the team with specifically skilled talent for each level of scaled growth and expanded marketing investment."

Kim lives the mantra, "Never let current available resources limit your big ideas. Go find the money." She raised over $15 million in five years to fund campaigns as they continued to see big opportunities to grow. When she and her leadership partners saw the opportunity to expand business into Walmart West, Sam's Club, and Costco, they raised funds for those specific efforts, then successfully delivered the growth. Using this same disciplined approach, Aspire is now launching in Canada.

"At a midsize company, there is more opportunity to be dynamic and nimble. But you can't play in the middle of the tennis court. If you think you can just coast, you are wrong. You need to always be anticipating the next growth and resource requirements. As a marketer or a member of the leadership team, you can actively drive strategy, general management, and M&A efforts—especially when you have a clear vision and value prop. When you work at a midsize, it's less bureaucratic to test and action interesting programs, as long as you manage to moderate risk as you do it."

> **For Next Gen:** When you are interviewing with a company, be sure to ask a variety of people about the organization's value proposition. What is ABC company's narrative? See if they know who they are and then check their answers against their website and public-facing collateral. Does everyone answer the same way?

UNDER ARMOUR OVERPERFORMS

Years ago, I was surprised by a company that knew their narrative and lived into it. I was in the toy industry, attending a seminar at the Licensing Expo. Between speakers, I introduced myself to the attendee sitting at my table, and he told me he was from Under Armour. I was so excited to meet someone from UA. At that time, I had recently acquired one of their new performance-material shirts that kept me warm during winter runs. I was obsessed with the new technology and had bought everyone on my Christmas list Under Armour garments. I shared all of this detail with the poor captive attendee and then asked him if he was at the show to buy licenses. You see, in my mind, their value proposition was that they made high-tech materials and garments to keep people warm. I imagined they would add a series of Mickey Mouse versions or Star Wars, etc.

He very nicely smiled back at me and said, "No. I'm here to license out the Under Armour brand." To which I thought, *Hmmmmm. Good luck with that, buddy!* However, he knew what their real narrative was. They were a lifestyle performance brand. Their narrative went way beyond shirt technology. I couldn't see it yet, but everyone at Under Armour apparently could.

Ten years later, they were one of the top licensed brands in the US.

> **For CEOs:** Test how your company expresses its narrative. Check the boilerplate of your press releases. Does that capture what you do and for whom? Ask a few people in different areas of the company how they describe the organization and its purpose. Look at your recruitment materials. Ask your best customer, "How would you describe our company?" Then see if the answers line up.

For CMOs: No matter how small the company, being able to powerfully tell your story is vital. I put this at the top of the "Marketing Imperatives to Get Right" list. A compelling story trumps a pretty PowerPoint, a handful of stats, and a bevy of influencers. Consider Spanx. Sara Blakely was a woman with a product that would make butts look better in clothes. And that story and product broke through. As for Bombas, they can deliver high-quality socks and help supply people in homeless shelters with these necessities. Shape the company's narrative.

A MIDSIZE COMPANY WITH A BIG-TIME NARRATIVE

One of my favorite stories is that of Build-A-Bear Workshop, the legendary toy company founded twenty-five years ago. Sharon Price John became CEO of Build-A-Bear in 2013, bringing with her two decades of experience in marketing, product development, and change management. She helped Build-A-Bear manage their narrative in a way that continues to have powerful results.

"A lot of the work," Sharon told me, "has been to pivot the company from a retail company that just happened to have built a powerful brand to a branded intellectual property company that just happens to have retail as one of its revenue streams. First, we had to understand our actual value. The actual value for Build-A-Bear happens to be the innate equity that's been built into this brand. So I asked myself, 'What are we going to do to build that infrastructure?'"

Sharon went right to the heart of the company's value proposition: the "heart ceremony." This is the symbolic moment in the Build-A-Bear experience when a guest puts a heart inside their new bear. It's not just a powerful moment for the guest but also for the Build-A-Bear employees. Sharon took the joy, trust, and love that are fundamental to this ceremony and used the value proposition to revitalize the brand and the company. Now, if you go to the Build-A-Bear website, you will find their narrative woven throughout, along with its mission to "add a little more heart to life."

"I've watched the DNA of this process permeate the minds and lives of all individuals involved," Sharon said. "Together, we've made Build-A-Bear a powerful brand and consistently profitable company, one heart ceremony at a time over the last twenty-five years, proving a lot can happen when you put your heart into it."

Here are a few more companies that stand out to me for having a clear value prop:

- **VTech**—Educational toys make learning fun.
- **Fresh Thyme**—Grocery stores offering fresh and healthy food at amazing values.
- **YETI**—Build products to improve your time in the wild.

- **Slack**—Be more productive at work with less effort.

- **Digit**—Save money without thinking about it.

- **HubSpot**—This is a great, easy-to-use CRM platform.

CHAPTER TWO

TEAM ORGANIZATION:
"I CAN'T TAKE ALL THIS CRAZY"

One of the most rewarding aspects of working for a midsize company is that people learn different skills that build their value as a professional and give them a strong sense of contributing to the organization's goals. Generally, there is enough budget to afford marketing assets, but there is also a need to make smart choices that will pay off. There is also a better opportunity to get to know more people at the company, collaborate with them, and make things happen.

To be clear, what I have just described is not the perfect situation for every marketer at every point in their career. **Marketers who thrive in midsize organizations must be prepared to show up every day—physically and/or mentally—because they enjoy the challenge.**

This story is what helped me frame the "midsize versus large corporation" concept in my head. As I mentioned in chapter 1, before grad school, I was working at a midsize company called P. Leiner. It was one of those classic "You need to show up every day, we have customers and they need their stuff; you need to have your head in the game" kind of places.

I was the new junior person, and I supported the West Coast sales team and customers. The East Coast person had all the major drug and big grocery chains. Her name was Dee, and she was a few years older than me. She was married. She had a toddler, and her husband was in law school. As if she didn't have enough stress in her life, she had to deal with the reality of LA traffic during her daily commutes. To make her life work, Dee would have to leave the office at a specific time, come hell or high water. She would take an exit off the 405, meet her husband, and they would transfer the baby from his car to her car so he could get to his night classes. Not everyone had laptops back then, so it wasn't that easy to work from home. She just made this hectic life work, day after day.

Then one day, she announced her resignation. I popped into her office and asked, "Dee, why are you going? You're so good at your job. I can't imagine this place without you."

She shut the door and said, "Look, it's a life stage thing. I can't take all this crazy. This job requires a lot. I'm going to a big company where I can be part of a larger team with a little more support. I can duck out early if I need to, and someone else can help pick up the slack on a tight day. I'm really good at this, but I have a lot of other things happening in my life. Right now, I can't kill it at work every damn day."

Mind: blown. I had so much respect for my colleague, but I could not get my head around what she was telling me. In retrospect, it was because I hadn't lived her life experience yet. I'd only had myself to take care of. And I had never worked at a larger company, so I had zero notion of this different workstyle environment Dee was describing. She was like, "This is what it is. And I'm opting out of here because I need something that looks more like *that*." Years later, I understood. And Dee went on to have a very impressive career.

WHO'S IN?

So who does work well in a midsize marketing department? Since the days when Dee and I worked together, both technology and work-life balance initiatives have made work in any environment more accessible for a whole lot more people. And with the COVID-19 pandemic, organizations are learning they can be much more flexible with work from home without sacrificing productivity.

Years ago, I learned a term from a CEO who was interviewing leadership team candidates. He was asking about their experience as a "player-coach." I immediately understood what he meant. The player-coach would still be handling a substantial number of functional tasks, in addition to managing and directing others to do the same. This is very different from micromanaging; the player-coach approach divides the work into piles, and the manager gets a pile of her own. When seeking managers for the midsize marketing department, definitely look for player-coaches.

I recently spoke with a CMO at a fintech company in high-growth mode. This company has a great value proposition: helping people manage their financial life. "When I joined the company," she said, "one of the early org changes was bringing in some new and more-senior staffers in key areas to augment the level of in-house expertise. These new hires had to be able to provide strategy—and also do the execution work. The interesting thing is that some of the new recruits had come from larger companies where they may not have done the execution work themselves in years because there were other junior staffers to help out. These team members were really the epitome of player-coach employees. Because as revenue grew, we were building out teams under them, and they were combining hands-on expertise with new staff management. The people who raised their hands for these positions knew what was needed of them, and they were looking for this kind of challenge and opportunity.

"Conversely, because we are growing quickly, I find the personnel who struggle are the ones who want the buttoned-up big-company process. Growth and scaling require flexibility and a more custom-built mindset."

Remember Kim Feil from chapter 1? On the day of our interview, she was in the midst of supporting the team to launch Aspire Healthy Energy Drinks at Costco. Not only was she equipping one hundred field ambassadors for the expansion, but she was also a couple minutes late to the call because she was loading product onto a truck that was headed to an Aspiring Artists music event. Now that's a player-coach!

I am often asked, "How do we write job descriptions to attract candidates who will be most successful in our marketing department?" In addition to the functional needs—digital advertising, PR, social media, CRM expertise, etc.—most job descriptions also mention "good communication skills" and "critical thinking skills." However, my observation is that in the interviewing process, few companies craft questions and conversations to assess these two criteria. It's fair to say they are glossed over and dumped in with "other duties as assigned."

A great marketing department will have a lot of cross-collaboration and integration within and outside the department. Staff will make creative and analytic choices to keep them customer-centric, ahead of the competition, and in sync with changing environments. This requires people with good communication skills—and communication has been a shape-shifting talent in the last few years. Professional communication today ranges from Slack, IM, Teams, and Zoom to email, texted emojis, and personal conversation. With COVID-19 sending millions of marketers to their home offices, communication processes have been expanded and tested. It's worth the time in an interview to ask specific questions about a candidate's communication style and the lessons they have learned through recent experiences.

"Critical thinking skills" sounds fairly generic, but in later chapters, we will explore how midsize companies can compete with much larger organizations—if they are smart. Team players who can think strategically, connect patterns, and contribute to different company efforts will enjoy a midsize company and will help an organization stay nimble. I like to ask candidates to tell me something really smart they observed or shared at their company that was not necessarily part of their job description.

Last, I have to say that the universal focus on diversity, equity, and inclusion (DE&I) has been such a boon to CMOs and CHROs as they think about staffing. Bringing in diverse backgrounds and skill sets has been proven to give organizations better results. Ethnic diversity is an important core measure; however, don't stop there. A team that supports a blend of gender, ethnicity, sexual orientation, age, and prior industry experience always stands the best chance of succeeding.

Lauren Tucker, founder and CEO of Do What Matters inclusion management consultancy, says, "Making money is easy. Making *more* money is hard. Organizations that prioritize inclusion are the ones who figure out how to grow and make more money." She went on to share, "It's all about the talent. Talent drives growth. In a positive culture, everyone feels safe, valued, and productive. People stay longer and grow their careers there.

"Conversely, in organizations where staff feel disengaged, there is a real cost to the company. A midsize company has everything to gain by cultivating an inclusive culture. And they may not be able to withstand the cost of a disengaged workforce. I strongly encourage the midsize organizations to **start** with inclusivity and watch the positive results."

One core question to consider when bringing people into a midsize company from a large organization is, Can they make the leap? There is a difference in resources and performance expectations; can they do it? It is a VERY important question to probe.

I was the CMO at a midsize manufacturing company. About eighteen months into our three-year growth push toward a potential company sale, our CEO resigned and left the company. The board from the private equity owners selected a new CEO from a Fortune 500 company—an individual who had never been a CEO before. I'm sure the board's assumption was his lack of CEO experience would be offset by his mega-company experience. It did *not* work that way.

It started with very visible cues that ran counter to the organization's culture. He chartered private jets to take the leadership team to our manufacturing sites when the custom—as it is with most companies—was to take commercial airlines. This exorbitant move was very tone-deaf to how the traditional midsize company operated. He then implemented other big-company staples: a personal admin versus shared resources, special tinted writing walls, an expensive downtown condo, and a new strategy staffer who answered only to him.

Though awkward, these gaffes may have been overlooked as early-days learning. What was unsupportable was the tone that came with the bigger organization credentials. It was clear that, in the new CEO's view, because the current staff came from a midsize organization, we were all less smart. The public berating and abusive behavior may have been part of the larger company culture (or maybe not), but it did not help our company's growth. Within six months of his arrival, 40 percent of the organization had left. The consecutive six-quarter revenue and profit growth trend tanked. It was a complete miscalculation of this individual's ability to transfer skills into a midsize organization.

> **For CEOs:** If you are in a growing company that is just beginning to integrate marketing into operations, you are probably evaluating how many roles you need to hire and the sequence of the hires. The holy grail is to prioritize for the greatest revenue impact and ROI.

For CMOs: Usually, a CMO moving into an organization will evaluate the existing marketing team. These are the key questions: Do we have the right roles? And do we have the right people in those roles? Defining the team structure, roles, and right people for a midsize company is key to successful growth. Occasionally, the CMO is starting from scratch. This usually happens in growth companies that have hit a point where product and sales alone can't keep up with the need, and the CEO has decided it's time to integrate a marketing team.

ROLES AND TEAM STRUCTURE TO MANAGE THE CRAZY

I have found myself in the "build the team" situation a couple of times. In the first instance, I started with a junior marketing generalist. I just needed someone to keep my head above water. She started with the most basic of marketing administration, but over the years, she discovered an element of the company she really enjoyed—licensing—and she became an expert in that area. My first hire's name was Kendra; she managed so much in the early days that I referred to her as "Super K"—and I still do to this day.

As that company grew, the complexity of our marketing needs was also growing. My boss at the time gave me some very good advice that I still value today. He told me, "You always need a strong #2. If you are lucky, you have a good #3 as well. But in order to survive, a strong #2 is a must." He was right. Once I hired someone who could understand not just a narrow scope of marketing deliverables but also the whole company strategy and annual plan, things started clicking.

For the company-wide team, there was now more than one person who could push marketing projects along. For me, there was personal freedom. I could go on vacation without having to stay glued to my computer. When I was home sick or with sick kids, I knew my "second" could keep progress moving. My boss had known from the start that I could only go for so long without that kind of support. So I try to implement his wisdom—and share it—wherever I go. The interesting part of having a second is that you need to *really* let go of some responsibilities and let the person own objectives, budgets, and core pieces of the business. Even more unnerving, you should really be training them to eventually replace you one day.

In midsize companies, marketing can play several different roles. In some, it is the hub of the organization and the center of branding, communications, and digital outreach to customers. In other companies, marketing plays more of a support role to sales or product development. And in some instances, marketing is purely lead generation to send to another department to close. Once you know what role marketing plays in the company, either through a legacy or strategic design, you can structure the team.

As you build out the structure, keep in mind **which roles facilitate revenue generation**—and prioritize them.

AGENCY VERSUS STAFF

This is an ongoing balance question. I refer to it as the decision to rent or own talent. And the answer will continue to evolve with the marketing department's growth. One secret for success is to augment the staff with agency help in a couple of key areas.

One: If there is a new project or initiative for which we—for a finite period of time—need a lot of resources and expertise we do not have in-house. A recent example is bringing on an outside agency to help get Salesforce Marketing Cloud implemented and start the transition from a legacy email system.

Two: If there is an area that is very dynamic that is not our core business. My primary example is a digital media agency. The rules behind the digital advertising platforms change rapidly, and I want my team to benefit from the knowledge an agency brings through their variety of clients. The agency is also "always on." There will always be somebody managing our adwords, etc., even when my staffer is out of the office. I always have adequate staff who manage the agency and have accountability for our digital performance.

Social media is an interesting question when it comes to in-house or agency. The "always on" aspect of an agency is certainly an advantage, especially as it relates to community management. But the content is usually so close to product and marketing that it can be difficult to keep an outside group up to speed with responses and brand voice.

In the end, the team structure should balance nimble highest return on investment and manage the "crazy" for the collaborative, critical-thinking high performers on your team.

TAKEAWAY TRUTHS

1. When hiring marketers for midsize organizations, look for critical thinkers who can operate as player-coaches.

2. Remember that a diverse team gives you a better chance at long-term success, and a consistent focus on inclusivity will keep your team productive and engaged.

3. Whenever possible, have a #2, and provide backup for everyone to manage the "crazy."

4. Find great agency help for marketing areas that are dynamic and not core to your business.

CHAPTER THREE

CROSS-COMPANY COLLABORATION:

THE GLUEY MIDDLE

Things weren't looking so good for VTech Learning Toys. They had lost their market position in the US to the new upstart, LeapFrog. Shortly after I joined the company, almost every retailer had removed VTech from the toy aisles. LeapFrog was fresh and cool, while the VTech brand seemed stodgy and out of touch. The VTech Toys team was Hong Kong-based, with the central product-development team located there; US product, marketing, and sales resided in Chicago. The entire VTech team knew that retailers thought we were finished. Buyers were not even giving us appointments until we had something "really new to talk about."

And that's where the story really began.

The Hong Kong product team had devised a video game system that could operate in a way similar to Xbox. However, competition with Microsoft, Nintendo, and Sony would be even more daunting than battling LeapFrog. Breaking with their tradition, the Hong Kong group looked to the US marketing team for consumer insight. We pointed out that American moms were being pressured to buy video games for their preschoolers and kindergarteners and that moms were not comfortable with the product and content for their young kids.

So we made a proposal: Let's take VTech's expertise in early childhood learning and put it on a game console for three- to six-year-olds. The Hong Kong team ran with it and created a chunky orange-and-purple console with an oversized joystick that we dubbed V.Smile. Game on.

The US product team came up with the tagline "Turn game time into brain time." The marketing team pitched the concept to all the kids licensing studios and signed on Disney, Scooby-Doo, Spiderman, and Care Bears for launch. The Hong Kong product team worked day and night with the US team to develop fun and educational software cartridges. Video game systems only work if they are supported with a library of games.

Then we made an outlandish commercial to promote V.Smile, in-aisle displays that retailers could use to demo the product, and a big PR plan. Our US chairman came out of retirement to work with the sales team and to prep us for the big pitch to retailers—at the North American International Toy Fair. We would see if we had something "really new to talk about."

The US VTech team—about ten of us, ranging in rank from president to admin—worked feverishly to set up an impressive showroom and hone the perfect demo and pitch in New York. In fact, everyone on the team from the US to Hong Kong had been working nonstop on the V.Smile. We had bet the ranch on this.

The verdict?

Walmart loved it, TRU wanted an exclusive on it, Target had to have it, and so forth and so on. The ten of us spent four days hunkered down in that showroom, bringing the work of an international team over the goal line. V.Smile became Toy of the Year, the revenues surprised even us, and VTech pulled off a complete turnaround to become one of the top toy companies— eventually overtaking and buying LeapFrog. I will never forget that sense of connectedness or the power of cross-functional teamwork.

Generally, at a toy company, the connection between product development, sales, and marketing is crucial. And in that respect, VTech is similar to most companies. Throughout that great experience, marketing was the glue that kept the product team, licensing work, and sales team connected.

I can attest that it was *not* all smooth sailing. There were differences of opinion about everything from the packaging to the pricing to the licensing contracts for the games and more. **But at**

a midsize company, ongoing partnerships between differ-ent departments are the key to success. At VTech, everyone focused on the end goal through a separate lens and a separate skill set. Bringing everyone together created success that led to momentum, and the momentum led to more financial success.

When I talk to other marketers and salespeople about expe-riences with connected teams and positive experiences, I hear some common themes to the VTech turnaround. First, people mention unifying against the competition and *not* one another. Having worthy competitors to beat is a proven motivator. In every category from tech and finance to hospitality and apparel, it's clear to see how competition drives all the players. Second, marketers and salespeople mention that having a common mar-ket goal (hitting $1 billion in revenue, winning a top-quality award, getting acquired, not going out of business) is a powerful motivator as well.

INTERNAL THEATER—DITCH IT

One of the big benefits of a midsize company is that the focus stays on beating the competition or the market. There is more opportunity for everyone to participate in the organization's success and to have their moment of contribution. While, of course, there are good examples of teamwork at larger compa-nies, it is harder to escape the gravitational pull of the organi-zation itself.

A friend who works for a large pharma company was recently bemoaning all of the slides and PowerPoint presentations she has to create to align multiple divisions within the company. They don't all want to participate in the enterprise-wide project she is charged with, so she spends days dealing with what I call "internal theater," or making presentations for internal audiences that don't necessarily drive external results.

Another marketing executive friend of mine used to work at a large automotive company where as many as a dozen senior leaders and important stakeholders were involved in approving a decision. As such, working teams spent weeks doing "political mapping" to assess where influencers stood in supporting their proposal. They developed action plans to get each player on board prior to the all-important Sales and Marketing Meeting—a large, formal, recurring venue where key marketing and product development proposals were approved. While dozens of staff were present, it was highly unusual for underlings (i.e., those who knew what was going on!) to speak. The purpose was apparently for senior leaders to render a verdict from on high.

"I remember when I was proud of all that hard work," my friend told me. "Back-channeling the real conversations in order to earn a rubber stamp at the big meeting. Looking back, it is painful to recall that professionals whose purpose was to innovate and launch new products spent so much time and energy conquering internal hurdles."

If you work for a big company, you are giving me an "Amen" right now. Right?

I have my own story to illustrate the reality of internal theater. During my time at Sears, the company still relied heavily on the revenue productivity of the circulars. Remember circulars? They were those inserts featuring weekly deals that came in newspapers. I would spend hours in rooms with other CMOs and marketing directors, debating who got what approved deal on which page and with how much space. It always amazed me—so many truly bright minds and substantial salaries locked in those rooms doing work that could have been delegated.

One of the circular review rooms was an auditorium with theater-style seating and a small stage. The meeting convener would project the pages being discussed on a large screen, cementing the image of internal theater in my mind. I definitely committed to winning the internal game. One December, the toy team I represented was in danger of losing pages to pajamas and snowblowers. So my boss (who was a very good sport) and I wrote and performed a rap song, making our case that we needed the space. Ugh. Circular space received; perspective lost.

MARKETING AS THE GLUEY MIDDLE

Even a small marketing team can be set up to get the most out of enterprise-wide teamwork. Some of the department connections are obvious; others are less so but can really unleash potential.

Part of the appeal of marketing at a midsize is that marketing is the center of the organizational hub and keeps the departments glued together.

Sales + Marketing should be like peanut butter and jelly. Each is better with the other. A sales team understands what customers want and don't want. That feedback to marketing helps make them stronger and more on target with messaging and product. Conversely, having on-point marketing materials all through the customer journey helps the sales process. I'm especially intrigued with some of the midsize software-as-a-service (SaaS) organizations I've interviewed. The way they connect sales to customer success teams to product development teams is masterful.

After Kim Feil left Walgreens and OfficeMax, small and midsize retail tech companies invited her to be on their advisory boards and boards of directors, and she joined a couple. "As a board member at PowerReviews," Kim told me, "I was able to observe the virtuous cycle of sales and marketing collaboration in a B2B service business. As the business development team cultivated a new customer, they focused on learning that customer's goals and needs. Business development then transferred that learning to the marketing and customer success team during customer sell-in and onboarding. This intentional knowledge transfer not only reduced churn but also made it easier to sell customers new services that were most appropriate for their needs. When you think about the full customer journey, you know that happy customers tend to buy more and try more services. So from sales to marketing, consistent collaboration pays off."

Marketing & IT. If the CMO has one bestie, it should be the CIO. Digital transformation and coordination are at the foundation of marketing today. Marketing and IT will need to be a united front to advance frictionless and productive customer interfaces. In midsize companies, the coordination of data, the customer-facing website, the CRM systems, and the email servers will vary from one place to the next. But they are all required for seamless customer experiences.

At every midsize company I have worked for in the past ten years, they have asked me to help with their digital transformation. What that *really* means has changed each year and with each company, but in every case, I've found that a close partnership between marketing and IT is the key to launching new channels and better digital marketing. Back in 2016, Gartner was reporting that CMOs were spending as much on digital purchases as CIOs. While the move to more cloud-based tools may have accelerated that trend, the expansion of even the most user-friendly marketing tools often needs IT coordination. Data security, platform coordination, and ongoing maintenance are just a few of the bare necessities IT will cover in this partnership.

> **For CMOs:** Really commit to a good working relationship with your IT or CIO counterpart. Chances are good his or her brain may work differently than yours, but that is a win. Together, your teams will rock your company and rival organizations much larger than yours.

Marketing & HR. In a midsize company, this can be the secret win. The marketing team, no matter how small, will be driving the company's positioning, branding, and visual image. The HR team, which in midsize companies is chronically lean staffed, could use that help.

Nancy, the CMO at a Chicago-based data analytics company, recounted a time when their HR department started recruiting at undergrad job fairs. Because they were understaffed and she wanted to understand how they presented at these venues, she sent one of her directors along to help. The director returned from the day mortified. When relaying this story to me, Nancy laughed and said, "We looked like the 'poor cousins' in a sea of polished recruiters at the university. No backdrop, no swag, no table cover, no substantial brand presence. Showing up like that screams, 'If you can't get a job anywhere else, try here.'"

Once Nancy was aware of the situation, it was simple to give that department the help it needed with online recruiting pages and in-person events. The HR team was great; they just did not think about the branding presence the way the marketing team did. Since that cross-divisional *aha* moment, the HR team asked Nancy's brand manager to review all of the recruiting materials. The net result was better conversion at in-person and online recruiting.

For Next Gen: Not 100 percent sure which aspect of business appeals to you? Working in a midsize marketing department is a great way to get insight into multiple functions within a business. Maybe you are more of a product person? Sales? HR? Find a company where marketing works with multiple departments to build your work experience as you answer these questions for yourself. Did you just graduate with an MBA and want to use more of your general management skills? A midsize company generally will provide that opportunity.

Marketing + Operations. I'm not kidding: This is where general management skills and cross-functional cooperation can make or break the bottom line. Consider the situation at EPI Products, when the marketing and sales team decided they would promote all of the skin care products for the month of February, urging retailers to load up at a discounted rate in December to be ready for the big advertised sale. Except neither marketing nor sales mentioned the promotion to operations. There was very little inventory of skin care product in stock, as it had been shipped to support the holiday season.

Oh, it gets worse. Shipping and ops did not tell sales that they were just canceling all of the orders where there was no inventory. So the sales team did not know the trouble was brewing until it was too late. Marketing moved forward with creating the commercial, which then had to be pulled as the company's communication problem was becoming their retail customers' problem. Consumers were looking for on-sale product that was not available on retailers' shelves.

A few months later, EPI Products ended up filing bankruptcy.

While that one incident was not the whole reason, it was indicative of what happens when the cross-functional teams aren't in sync.

The ops + marketing connection was less apparent to me initially at the building products company. It was a very manufacturing-driven company, and I would sit week after week at the CEO's staff meeting, listening to details about factory output and production issues. The upside is that I got the opportunity to learn a lot about production and factory KPIs and what products would be available when.

Then one day, the theoretical advantage of having marketing connected to ops became real. We found out that our Midwest factory and warehouse were having extreme issues keeping up with demand and shipping to our customers. We discovered exactly *how* extreme when the social media manager found a Facebook group consisting of truckers complaining about the daylong waits they faced in trying to get loaded up. The details of the Facebook page opened up a much bigger conversation within the leadership team. We were unaware of the extent the plant was struggling to keep up. Ultimately, the warehouse was not able to get ahead of the issue with the legacy inventory and shipping software system they were using. Fixing their infrastructure was an expensive problem.

While enterprise shipping systems are *way* outside of my wheelhouse, I could still easily lean into the "fix it" collaboration. First, I looked at how much of our advertising we could cut. There was no need to stimulate more demand for something that couldn't be shipped. Those funds were then redirected to my colleagues to help resolve a more foundational issue for our joint success. My CFO, who had come from a background of both large and midsize companies, joked that he had never seen a marketing department hand over so much budget without a fuss. We agreed it was because I had been included in the conversations and could see the whole picture. That's what I like about the midsize environment.

For CEOs: Are your CMO and marketing team linked with your other departments? How can you facilitate the interconnectedness that promotes enterprise thinking versus functional group concerns? Are there clear handoffs and systems that help promote the collaboration?

TAKEAWAY TRUTHS

1. Marketing at a midsize adds the most value when that team is collaborating with all departments.

2. The CMO's success is linked to the CIO's. A tight marketing + IT connection is critical for digital marketing.

3. A CEO at a midsize can unlock potential by establishing practices and a culture of cross-functional collaboration.

CHAPTER FOUR

THE TRUTH ABOUT BRANDING:

FROM THE OUTSIDE IN

When I come into a midsize organization and start to understand the brand, I approach the task as an outsider—a customer. First, I start taping onto my office walls every marketing flier, ad, packaging, or post I can find. It quickly becomes uncomfortable for people who walk into my office because they see the company as the public sees them. All of the old, outdated stuff that never got cleaned up? I tape it up like an NCIS crime scene room—all of the different logos, fonts, tones, colors, calls to action, QR codes, spokespeople, and hashtags, all in one big visual review. At Sylvan Learning, my exterior office walls were glass, so my process was especially obnoxious. Finally, my boss, the CEO, said, "I think I'm getting the point. I want to cry every time I walk by this. You're going to have to take it down."

Of course, I took it down. But it helped me to realize, Okay, this is what we look like. This is what our brand looks like at this snapshot in time—not to *us,* but to other people who see us.

Which is exactly why **it's vital that you look at your brand from the outside in.**

The OG guru of marketing, Kellogg's professor Philip Kotler, maintains the classic take on branding. While talking about the new edition of the *Marketing Management* textbook, he said, "In the old days, a brand simply told you what the product is and does and how it's priced. But today, a brand is the company's promise to deliver a specific benefit that addresses a particular need of its customers." IMHO, Kotler is always right on these matters, and branding, when done well, can help deliver that value.

If you are at a midsize organization, you are probably rebranding, refreshing the brand, or creating a brand for a new strategic piece of the business. Or perhaps you are creating a brand architecture that works because you have acquired new companies or product lines, and you need something that makes sense. Outside of marketing, rebranding is frequently regarded as a design exercise. You simply change the logo, add a new tagline, and adjust the color palette. And that *could* be one approach.

On the other hand, rebranding can be a cornerstone of bigger change management in an organization that is growing or shifting gears. The first step is to define why you are rebranding and to get leadership alignment on why this work will ultimately benefit the business. It's most efficient to start with the end business goal in mind. The next step is to get *real* about your budget for the process.

There are some great agencies across the country that can help with the branding process but, depending on what you need and what kind of shop you select, this work can cost a boatload of money. Investing in the brand is generally a smart idea, but if the budget is tight, you may need to consider a scrappy hybrid approach.

Are you nodding along, saying, "Tell me about the scrappy approach"? Here's the truth about branding: you have options. Most branding or rebranding undertakings use the classic four steps: **Discover, Define, Develop, Deliver.** This is the basic approach every top-dollar branding agency will take you through. Your marketing team can take on some or all of these steps, depending on your budget and staff skill sets.

Discover. Research. As much as possible. Beyond the wall of pictures. Understand what customers think of your brand. What do noncustomers think of the brand? What do your employees think? How do you line up with your competitors? How does the brand sound in communications? Outline all the research you will need to make informed decisions. And don't gloss over the internal company work; the brand will have to emanate from the inside out. No matter how brokeass your budget is, the research is critical and may be the area in which you invest in outside help. The more quantitative and qualitative information you get, the better decisions you can make.

The output should illustrate your current brand equity and the brand's fit with the business strategy. This is your snapshot in time and starting point.

Define. Analyze the data. Look at the feasible positions for the company and the brand. Decide how far away you can move from the current position, and use the data from discovery to support your rationale. The data should show how your brand is positioned among competitors and if there is white space that you should claim in the category. In several past brand refreshes, my team has found brand archetypes to be quite useful in the Define process. Brand archetypes are character types that embody different qualities that are universally recognizable to most people. (The hero, the everyman, the innocent, etc.) Your research data will show which archetypes represent your brand *in the eyes of your customers and employees.*

For CMOs: I keep repeating the need to reference the data. Otherwise, a branding exercise can become bogged down with internal opinions versus customer data. Avoid the living hell of the circular brand conversation. I was once bogged down for over two months trying to advance the brand positioning process with a leadership team. A couple of well-meaning stakeholders were very attached to some legacy ideas, and while the rest of the team understood the gap that the data illustrated, a couple of them could not. To their credit, with unwavering consistency, they tenaciously defended their opinions in our work sessions. (Read: we spent weeks covering the same territory.) Finally, the data conversation prevailed, and the CEO indicated it was time to keep moving forward.

The data will also help you formulate "From — To" statements that tie branding back to the business strategy. For illustrative purposes, let's say an enterprise—Fishy Business—is in the fishing category. Their discovery research may have shown that the brand is known for bait, convenient hours, and knowledgeable staff. If the business strategy is to grow by offering higher-end rods and equipment, the desired positioning would need to change. One possibility is:

From	**To**
The best bait people in the business	The preferred place for the savvy fisherman

There will probably be a few possible brand position statements that could work. At this point, the marketing team would want to pressure-test the positioning with internal leadership, an employee focus group, and some customers. It's also a great idea to test the positioning against your value prop (see chapter 1) and against a typical customer journey. Once there is alignment on the brand positioning that you are driving to, make sure to capture it in a strategy document. I prefer using a brand ladder, but it is critical to have a one-pager that says it all.

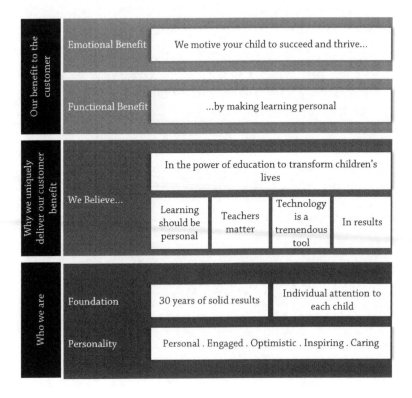

Our benefit to the customer	Emotional Benefit	We motive your child to succeed and thrive…			
	Functional Benefit	…by making learning personal			
Why we uniquely deliver our customer benefit	We Believe…	In the power of education to transform children's lives			
		Learning should be personal	Teachers matter	Technology is a tremendous tool	In results
Who we are	Foundation	30 years of solid results		Individual attention to each child	
	Personality	Personal . Engaged . Optimistic . Inspiring . Caring			

At this point in the process, everyone is tired of the strategy, analysis, and talking. They want to create.

Develop. Here's where marketing decides on the elements needed to make the brand platform real. Ideally, start with a manifesto—brief or long. Next up is the tagline, which is probably different from the positioning statement. Other new assets the marketing team may take on include the following: new logo, new voice and tone, new advertising campaign, and reworked key touchpoints, including website, social platforms, etc. Prior to launch, the marketing team needs to create a new brand guidelines document. It should incorporate everything partners would need to know to understand the brand and create assets that are 100 percent in lockstep with the new brand positioning. This is the time to decide how many assets will be needed to effectively launch the brand refresh.

> **For CMOs:** Do you use your existing creative director for a brand refresh, or not? The risk in leaving the new creative refresh with your existing creative director is that you might get only a slight revision of the brand's old look. If you want a revolutionary change versus an evolutionary change, you will want the new creative direction to come from an external source. Most good creative directors can participate as a stakeholder in dialing in the new brand look from an agency. And then the creative director can lead the rollout of the brand using the refreshed brand guide.

Deliver. Every good brand launch or refresh needs a communication plan. The plan starts with the employees. They have to be excited first, and this branding refresh may cause them to rethink their contributions through a new filter. The rest of the rebranding communication plan moves outward one circle at a time: employees to boards, to vendors, to other stakeholders, and then to the customers and general public.

The next very unglamorous part is the creation of the no-holds-barred laundry list: literally every item that will need to be refreshed with the new branding. It is key to have this from the get-go and plan the transformation of every asset to reflect the new branding and voice. In most midsize organizations, you can't afford to change everything on launch day. Your accounting partners may have heart palpitations if you suggest trashing all inventory of existing collateral and replacing every building sign across the country. A deliberate process of prioritizing what is needed for launch, and what becomes longer-tail conversion, helps to manage cost. This is the very nuts-and-bolts work that determines the overall success of a brand refresh.

For Next Gen: If you are a more junior member of a midsize marketing department, the odds are good that you end up managing the laundry list of brand changes. It's not a curse! It's the business equivalent of a spring cleaning. And at the end of the process, you will know where every refreshed document and asset resides. People have become senators with less power than that. Seriously, it is a great project in conjunction with your creative team (or person) to combine operations with design and branding skills.

BRANDED HOUSE OR HOUSE OF BRANDS?

Many midsize companies grow through acquisition. This approach creates integration work across all functional areas, but marketers have the specific challenge of creating a branding structure that works for the newly forged company.

The question for the acquiring company quickly becomes, **Are you a branded house or a house of brands?**

I was working with a company that made premium composite decking and railing. Originally, the company was called AZEK. When they bought their competitor, TimberTech, they changed the company name to CPG International so it could equally support both of the brands. It turned out to be a suboptimal choice for company branding. First, the company was not CPG (consumer products and goods) nor was it international. But that quirk aside, it had created a funding challenge for itself. When we first met, they explained that they were frustrated that brand recognition was not significantly growing, neither for their AZEK nor their TimberTech-branded product. They had chosen to be a house of brands.

When you think of a house of brands, it brings to mind Gap. They have the Gap brand, Banana Republic, Athleta, and Old Navy. Meta has Facebook, Instagram, WhatsApp, and others. Each of these brands has either a distinct audience from the other brands or strong enough brand equity that it made sense to preserve them independently. *And they generated enough revenue to justify supporting the individual brand.*

The AZEK and TimberTech brands were not generating enough cash to justify building both of them. And they appealed to a very similar audience.

A branded house would be a company that absorbs all acquired companies under their own master brand. The obvious advantage is that they all benefit from the strength and advertising budget of the master brand. Big company examples of this strategy are Virgin, Amazon, and Apple.

CPG International had a robust enough marketing budget to grow one brand, but they needed some branding architecture to separate the AZEK and the TimberTech product lines. They also found that some building contractors were very brand loyal to the product they were most familiar working with. After careful consideration, we chose the branded house hybrid. First, the firm's name was changed to the AZEK Company. The AZEK product line remained the same, and the TimberTech product line became TimberTech by AZEK.

In a midsize company, making budget-rational decisions is critical. Leadership has to be realistic about how much time and cash is needed. It takes sustained investment over several years to get your target customer to recognize your brand and know what it stands for. I've seen plenty of growth-by-acquisition companies ignore their branding problem, and it drags on for years. Or they fail to differentiate the brands by retail channel or audience. It's a wasted opportunity to leverage a marketing budget. Either justify the expense of keeping the new brand(s) or build your branded house.

LIVING THE BRAND

As I mentioned earlier, sometimes a brand refresh can help galvanize broader organizational change. The American Lung Association had been operating as eight separate charters across the country. In 2017, when they came together as one organization, there were eight different versions of the American Lung Association trying to coexist. I had the pleasure of joining the organization in 2018 after the big operational shifts were done and some of the dust had settled. The other reality in 2018 was that this important heritage brand had not been refreshed in over one hundred years, and it was due for a tune-up that reflected its current place in public health.

This is where the adage "If you want to go fast, go alone. If you want to go far, go together" came into play. In order to knit these eight separate ALAs into one organization, we formed a branding committee that included board members and staff from different functional areas and geographies. We spent a good year going through the first three Ds (Discover, Define, and Develop). We partnered with Edelman, as they knew not only how to shepherd the brand refresh but also how to use the brand positioning work to finish the change management that had begun with the reorganization. All staff were invited to answer questionnaires, many stakeholders were able to contribute, and all leadership committed to the process and the delivery.

Call it serendipity, but in the end, the process reflected the outcome of our branding. We defined ourselves as the trusted champions of lung health: always optimistic, inclusive, and looking for solutions that will bring about our vision of a world free of lung disease.

There were some particular topics that surfaced with a heritage brand. The big question is, How far do you move from the OG brand? We were very thoughtful about the choices because we did not want to lose any of the constituents or donors who currently trusted the American Lung Association. We felt confident in our selected voice, architecture, and positioning, but we spent a lot of time on the visuals. In the end, we kept the double-barred cross that had been part of the logo lockup for a century. But we imbued it with meaning. Each of the three lines represents part of our mission: education, advocacy, and research. And then we changed all of the harsh red coloring to trusted champion blue—the color of a clean sky and the feeling of a deep breath.

Yes, we changed the logo, the voice, and the color palette, but we also finished changing an organization.

Whether you just refreshed your one hundred-year-old heritage brand or wrestled your gaggle of straggling brands into an architecture that makes sense, when you get to delivery time, you need to live the brand. This is an inside job. It starts with leadership and the marketing team, and it's built on the brand's promise and meaning.

This is not the time to be bashful. Put the manifesto in the HQ lobby. Put it on every desk or laptop if y'all work remotely. If you have a common work building, think about how your space should look. Think about how your brand should sound when your service team is talking to customers. Is the tone of your social media matching the brand voice? This is where it is helpful to have a cross-divisional team rolling out the brand. The way the company looks, acts, and relates should all flow back to the brand.

Making this happen in a midsize company can really galvanize teams from the different functional areas. It reinforces a sense of community. And if you are cut out for this scrappier approach to branding, it's actually a lot of fun.

For CEOs: There are numerous articles and books that discuss the value of brands and the increased value of companies that invest in their brands. While your CMO and marketing team may be driving this process, stay involved. Ask questions. Align yourself with the decisions. Also, be honest about the budget and the bandwidth to do rebranding work internally or externally.

TAKEAWAY TRUTHS

1. Always look at your brand from the outside in.

2. There are many ways to take on a brand refresh, but investing in research will always keep the work grounded to the customer and business outcomes.

3. Make budget-realistic choices when deciding whether you are going to be a branded house or a house of brands.

4. A brand refresh can be an opportunity for change management when an organization is at an inflection point.

CHAPTER FIVE

WHO IS YOUR CUSTOMER?:

THE SYLVAN EDGE

Hallmark Cards had an amazing research department. It was fully staffed with smart, insightful people who used qualitative, quantitative, primary, and third-party research and POS analytics. And they *knew* the customers and customer segments.

One year, the creative group on the valentine team thought Hallmark should have a fresh, new Valentine's Day look featuring purple and orange for the cards and gifts. Poor buggers—they were sick to death of red and pink and assumed everyone else in the world was as well. The research team told them that the customer for this holiday is more traditional, and this proposed color palette change could go very, very badly. But the "purple and orange" creatives persisted, and valentine sales fell harder than a poached rhino that year.

Needless to say, Hallmark is a big private company, one that can easily recover from a valentine-sized bump in the road. But I still look back on that research group and think, *Wow! What a luxury to have that resource.* The research crew were the ones who taught me the phrase, "Don't scorn the corn!"—meaning corny cards still sell *so* much better than the cutting-edge trendy cards. This was verified by POS data as well. They also taught me that monkeys are a sure bestseller in almost every card category; if sales are slumping in Walmart everyday cards, push in more religious Precious Moments; and that customers buy birthday cards that match the recipient's personality but buy boxed Christmas cards (remember those?) that reflect their own personality. This is an advantage of working at big companies: you get an extra layer of smart people to tell you about your customer.

But at Hallmark, creating greeting cards was a healthy and very profitable business in those days. And individual business groups thought they could afford to ignore good input from an independent research department. For those of you in big, siloed organizations, you know the dynamic I am talking about. It's too easy to lose sight of "in service to the customer" while negotiating workflow between departments.

CUSTOMER CENTRICITY IS
THE CORNERSTONE

At a midsize company, knowing your customer is a vital maxim that never goes out of style. Customer centricity is the cornerstone of marketing, especially if you believe the role of any company is to create value for its customers. In the words of Kellogg's professor Alexander Chernev, "Marketing is all about understanding, designing, communicating, and delivering value [to the customer]. This is the foundation of marketing strategy."

Today, there are tools that make it even easier to learn who your customers are through data analytics. And that knowledge is power. It helps your team dial in product features and benefits, hone your messaging, select your media channels, and assess your pricing. And for a manufacturer, relevant customer information helps to secure shelf space—real or virtual—with retailers.

At VTech, the midsize toy manufacturer, we were able to secure retail space at Walmart, Target, Toys "R" Us, and Amazon by telling them not only who our customers were but also what they were thinking and how they would react in the retailers' aisles and online space. While Walmart knows plenty about its shoppers, our buyers would not know as much as we did about a mom's mindset when she is thinking about an educational toy for her child or great Christmas presents for her whole shopping list.

VTech listened to their customers by investing in a lot of qualitative research. We clocked serious hours behind the mirrored glass, listening to focus groups of moms talking about their kids and toys. But the real insights came from their dialogue around their challenges, hopes, and fears about parenting. Spoiler alert: Everyone wants their children to be happy and successful. I ate about 1,000 pounds of M&M's during those listening sessions, but, damn, I know a lot about moms now. So do the product, creative, and operations people who were listening with the marketing team. I also know that in the eyes of all those moms, not one of them has an "average" child. And who knew that *so* many people have "gifted" children?

It was during these mom conversations that a theme emerged about their wanting to be popular with their young kids and give them video games and still wanting them to have learning toys that would make them more successful in school. This gave rise to V.Smile, which we discussed in chapter 3: the video console that turned game time into brain time—the toy that would sell hundreds of thousands of units and win Toy of the Year. In the end, V.Smile solved a problem for the customer.

For Next Gen: Get invited to any kind of customer interface, including focus groups, mixers, and data reviews. Be there. The insights you absorb from listening to those you serve are invaluable. They can also help as you connect with cross-functional teams and projects. Tie your ideas back to the customer's needs.

Knowing your customer is just as critical in B2B businesses. Back in 2017, I had hired an agency that specialized in paid search, and they had just started expanding into programmatic digital advertising and paid social as well. They were voted that year one of the top small agencies in the country. The account people were scrappy, smart, customer focused, and excellent. Every four weeks, the president, Zach, would call me just to see if we were happy and to ask what was on our horizon.

Unsurprisingly, the next year, they won in the top Medium-Sized Agency category. That total company focus on customer satisfaction paid off. Zach's agency was bought by another agency, and then he merged that digital agency with three others. Today, his group is too big for my company to hire, but I'm looking for the next Zach. And I think it may be Darwin. Don't even ask, or Darwin's company will grow too big for my business too!

THE LADY OF THE HOUSE

In the AZEK Building Products company, they had been very sure that their customer was a man. And they were partially right. Almost all of the contractors who built the decks were men. But these contractors sold to homeowners. When I was brand new at the company, the CEO sent me on a road trip to talk to scores of contractors across the country and learn the business. I asked them all, "Who makes the purchasing decision on the deck color and materials?" They all replied the same: the female head of the household.

Okay, what they really said was, "The lady of the house." One contractor from Atlanta told me, "You know, just once, I'd like to have one of these ladies ask me for your product by name. I prefer your product; I really do—but they don't know your name yet."

When I brought this insight back to HQ, all of the sales team members agreed that it made sense to them. So that year, in addition to the contractor-focused messaging, we went with a very fashion-forward print and digital campaign targeted to the ladies of the house. It was a huge departure in the building product industry, and it did help product sell through.

The Atlanta contractor did call me back. He said that people were not asking for us by name yet, but one homeowner pulled up the ad from *Southern Living* and said, "I want this stuff." We took it as a win.

> **For CEOs:** If you are onboarding a new CMO, sending her on a get-to-know-the-customer road trip is a fantastic idea. This looks different for every business, but the foundation and the relationship-building are worth the time invested.

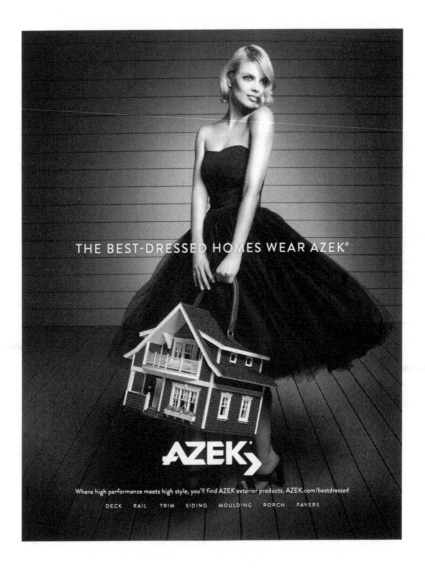

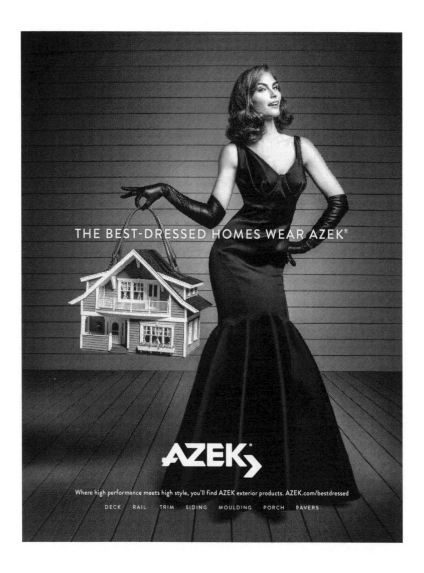

THE BEST-DRESSED HOMES WEAR AZEK®

AZEK⟩

Where high performance meets high style, you'll find AZEK exterior products. AZEK.com/bestdressed

DECK   RAIL   TRIM   SIDING   MOULDING   PORCH   PAVERS

DIGITAL DETECTIVE WORK

With today's digital tools, even smaller companies can get great insights into their customers. By leveraging a company's email database, e-commerce customers, social media followers, and even website visitors, there is a bounty of information that can paint a picture in aggregate of who your customer is. Depending on your business model, you can also understand what they value—promotions, innovation, relevant content. I subscribe to a digital music service, and they noticed I listen to a lot of Imagine Dragons. (Don't judge me!) So they sent me an email with the band's concert schedule for this year and a link to buy tickets. It's borderline creepy, but because it has value to me, I did not mind. I'll be the one singing "Follow You" at the top of my lungs in Boston this summer.

Using aggregated data appends really helped us understand a customer segment at the American Lung Association as well. We had assumed that our climate change and clean air work was appealing to a younger demographic. We hypothesized that Gen Zers and millennials were the ones coming to our site, jumping on our advocacy bandwagon, and even donating.

A little digital detective work proved us all wrong. We worked with a data partner to investigate every "clean air" constituent record we had from any of our digital channels. Agencies with data platforms compare your digital records to their databases that are aggregates of licensed data, census data, tax returns, social listening, phone records, purchasing behavior, and more.

The result? We found that the average age of our climate change and clean air constituent was fifty-two years old. The surprise is that they were really appreciating the young climate change activists and influencers' content that we had assumed would be consumed by a younger audience. This knowledge helps us determine what we should do to keep the older core audience and what may work to attract new customer segments.

Digital tools have also made it much less expensive to launch quantitative studies in which targeted respondents answer online. These reports can either deliver comprehensive background on your customer persona or, with research services such as Suzy, help you answer discrete questions about their opinions on a product or topic.

"The foundation of effective marketing is knowing your customer," said Matt Britton, founder and CEO of Suzy. "It's even more important for midsize companies with tight budgets to have good information and insights before making expensive product, advertising, media, or messaging decisions. Research tools have come a long way in the last decade, and organizations of every size can invest in fast and critical insights."

MAKE NEW FRIENDS, BUT KEEP THE OLD

Most midsize companies I work with have aspirations of growing, often to that elusive $1 billion mark. I recently spoke to a CEO of a premiums company—you know, cups and pens with company names on them. They had about $250 million in revenues, and he was explaining to me how they were going to hit $1 billion in three years. I may have been one of the first to ask him, "My, that is impressive. How are you planning to do that?" Because he did not have an answer.

For those *with* a plan, a common growth strategy is to expand audience segments to help grow revenues. The marketing team's challenge is, How do you keep delivering value to the current customer base while reaching out to the new segment? Through the CMO Collective, I met another CMO who shared with me her new-customer journey.

My longtime friend Mary Ellen Dugan is the former VP of global marketing for Indeed, the number one job site worldwide. She shared the following example of expanding a customer base without dropping your core customer.

"Indeed is a great example of a company that was able to expand through a new customer base. Since its inception, Indeed had an unwavering focus on the job seeker and the enterprise (large company) clients who often had the most roles to fill. As you may have figured out—don't worry; I won't tell—Indeed is free to the job seeker. Indeed's engagement efforts ensure that job seekers have a good experience, but the business model is to charge companies to promote open positions through pay-per-click advertising. Larger companies with robust recruitment budgets were more likely to find investing in Indeed's services a justifiable business expense.

"So the core business was built around this desirable business segment. However, Indeed realized that the small-business segment (SMB) was the fastest growing sector in hiring companies, and they focused on developing a strategy to serve this segment without disrupting their healthy enterprise business.

"Their growth strategy was successful. Today, you can go to their website and find 'Indeed for Enterprises,' which invites you to join the 96 percent of Fortune 500 companies that are using Indeed. And then it showcases a range of its up-leveled products that have been developed and honed for the large customer. Similarly, you can go to their 'Indeed for Small Business' page, where a more modest set of "right-sized" tools and talent sourcing options are featured. The product offerings and marketing were built on a deep knowledge of what was important to the customer and how to reach a new segment without diluting the service or satisfaction to the original base.

"Within tech software, there are many examples of companies that start with the small-business segment and then want to pivot to capture the enterprise customer. The allure is the promise of more revenue per customer, but the switch does not always work. Companies need to be realistic about their product scaling to the needs of a different customer—especially an enterprise client. What's the mantra? *It's all about the customer!*"

THE SYLVAN EDGE

In many cases, your core customer base may be open to new products from your company. Sylvan Learning had a new product idea but also had all the challenges most midsize companies face: a limited budget, a small bandwidth, a narrow brand, and a somewhat skeptical franchisee base. However, we had the benefit of a CEO—Jeff Cohen—who embraced innovation and promoted cross functional collaboration. Their product idea was to offer a STEM curriculum that featured coding and robotics for kids. The product team had partnered up with Lego for the STEM curriculum and the products that supported it.

However, one of the obstacles was the Sylvan brand. It was really known for remediation—tutoring for kids struggling to read and understand math—not for accelerated learning. Also, the franchisee's business model was built on teachers teaching a few students at a time, not executing group classes. As if the branding and operational challenges were not enough, the financial reality raised a few questions with the franchisees. To be market competitive, the STEM classes needed to be priced at a rate that made them considerably less profitable than the more intensive tutoring engagements.

This is where the midsize company collaboration showed what was possible. The breakthrough was really based on knowing the customer. It started with a New Jersey franchisee, Antony, pointing out that every afternoon and evening, he had moms and kids in his waiting room, hanging out until the one sibling was done with tutoring. Antony was also game for piloting the STEM classes at his site, just to understand who would show up and how the group classes worked. He became a valuable partner in figuring out the customer for the new STEM product.

While we kept saying the tutoring product and the acceleration product had two different customers, he finally came back and said, "I'm not so sure. I recruited my first STEM students by asking my existing base of moms if they knew anyone who might be interested in Lego robotics." They brought in their scout troops, their child in tutoring, and their child's siblings. (Yes, the kids who had been hanging out in the waiting room.) The good thing about the Sylvan mom customers is that they already appreciated how *amazing* these educators are. The Sylvan NPS (net promoter score) ratings are truly off the charts.

The more we talked with Antony, the more we thought, *Why wouldn't we invest in a product that brought so many new kids into the Sylvan centers?* Even if the STEM classes are less profitable, once the moms meet the high-quality educators at the Sylvan centers, some percentage of them will also have kids who need the higher-profit tutoring.

So the coding and robotics classes became a recruiting tool for families who might also need the higher-priced tutoring. We took Antony's approach for recruiting kids for his STEM pilots and flipped the narrative. The customer—the mom—was the same.

But the brand still created a barrier to attracting moms who were seeking accelerated learning classes, such as coding and robotics, for their kids. We did not have the budget to build a whole new brand, so we found a good hybrid solution. We launched Sylvan Edge: the suite of fun STEM classes built to give kids an edge. It had a whole new "edgy" look, but it still fit under the umbrella of Sylvan branding.

More importantly, the group sessions, the Lego robotics, and the cool curriculum gave the Sylvan centers an energy boost. Marketing VP (now CMO) Amy Przywara was instrumental in this whole process. Once Sylvan Edge was piloted, she developed an internal communication plan that helped the franchise team see the program potential. At launch, over 60 percent of the franchisees adopted Sylvan Edge at their centers, and they all found initial success filling the first classes by talking to their existing moms. Eventually, they filled more tutoring seats from the families that showed up for Sylvan Edge.

This brand launch was truly a combined effort of franchisees and staff. It was marketing, product development, operations, strategy, and finance noodling through a pile of challenges. There were a few moments along the way when we wondered if we should chuck it. But in the end, we found a new way to expand the business. This is the kind of collaboration and teamwork I find more frequently at midsize marketing departments.

For CMOs: The question of who is the customer (in this last example, the question was, The mom or the child?) helps to define the marketing strategy. It's the difference between looking for two different moms and looking for a mom with children who may have different needs.

TAKEAWAY TRUTHS

1. Know your customer.

2. Know your customer.

3. Always refer to #1 and #2.

SECRETS AND STRATEGIES FOR SUCCESS

DIGITAL MARKETING— ECOSYSTEMS:

WHERE DAVID CAN TAKE GOLIATH

One thing about digital marketing is it levels a lot of playing fields. You can be a midsize company and your website could look as sharp as, or better than, that of a large organization. An on-point digital marketing game can be a solid competitive advantage. I think this is one of the reasons more early-career marketers are attracted to smaller and midsize companies. **You don't have to be a big company to have a great digital presence.**

This really gives smaller organizations the opportunity to be disruptors. And the options to build affordable, high-functioning sites and apps continue to grow. Whenever I embark on a digital marketing transformation with a company, the work starts with the website and builds out from there.

When talking about websites, I refer to them as "conversion machines." They need to convert on two levels: hearts and minds.

First, they must convert how the viewer feels about the brand. The design, user experience (UX), and content need to deliver on the brand narrative.

Second, they need to convert on the business's key purpose: e-commerce purchase, subscription, donation, lead generation, etc. This is such an important step in designing a digital transformation. It's most efficient to start with the "conversion machine" and work backward. Once the conversion goals are clear, then site design can begin.

When it comes to optimizing a website, either a start-from-scratch project or a refresh, I prefer to have an in-house team of IT and digital marketers work together and hire an agency to help with the lift. At most midsize companies, there are two "owners" of the website. The IT group owns the functionality, APIs, and data flows, while the marketing team owns branding, content, traffic, and conversions. The division of duties varies depending on the business and the staff's skill sets. But the IT team and the marketing team usually come to the project with a different set of questions.

One of the first questions is if the legacy back end, the content management system (CMS), is working well for your needs.

With older systems, it could be very difficult to work with the CMS, and it limits who can update the website. That was the case for us at the American Lung Association. One of the requirements of the CMS was that it should be intuitive enough for several of our digital marketers and content developers to access and use. We had been hamstrung with an older CMS that required our IT team to update many types of content. That constraint caused bottlenecks, and we were using higher-priced FTEs to perform tasks that could be spread out among many team members.

A CMS can vary in cost and complexity. Plan to do a lot of research on this decision before leaping into the site redesign. This is where I appreciate having an agency recommend one or more redesigns based on needs and forecasted web traffic. The vendors and the offerings in this space change fairly frequently, so I value an agency that lives in the category and can help with the appropriate selection. One of my favorite resources for sizing up options is G2.com.

> **For CMOs:** In many midsize companies, the leadership team will not be excited to hear about the CMS and how important it is to a successful site. You have to impress upon them the value of the back-end functionality and not just how good the home page looks.

CENTER OF THE ECOSYSTEM

Before you start designing the site itself, you will want to work with your team to map out the company's total digital ecosystem. Usually, you will be setting up your website to be the center of your ecosystem so customers can move from your primary site to your other digital platforms. In some cases (Noom, Reframe, Club Pilates, Calm), the goal is to move customers from an informational website to an app where most of the interaction will take place. Other platforms to consider include linked training sites, partner sites, and all the social platforms.

Your overall digital ecosystem is like the "you are here" map. This is also helpful when there are future discussions to add sites or platforms that live outside of the primary website. A prime example of this is an e-commerce presence on Amazon, eBay, or other sites.

After making the CMS decision and completing the ecosystem mapping, the next step is working through the customer journey on your site. What do customers need from your site? What do you want them to do? This is another part of web redesign in which I find an agency to be very helpful in asking all of the business-requirement questions up front. Then the agency will combine that information with your branding, best-in-class functionality, and a clear hierarchy that works for SEO and conversion.

For most redesigns, we ask agencies to present three options for what the site architecture could look like, basic wireframe options, and design looks. Usually, for the design looks, a home page and a core content page will be enough for the staff team to make a decision. This is a "measure twice, cut once" moment. Have the IT and digital marketing teams really study the options. Have key stakeholders look at the options. And above all, consider the customer journey for your website. Will it be a great UX? Will it deliver the conversion rate you expect? Don't rush the critical-thinking time on this step before you start to build out the new site.

Given that we are talking about midsize company budgets, I suggest that the arrangement with the web design agency be to get you started with core pages for your site but then to create templates for your team so they can create more content pages on their own. I've worked with sites that have anywhere from sixty to twenty-two thousand pages, so it is paramount to decide how the content will get migrated from the legacy site, how much content will be new, and what content doesn't spark joy any longer and can be discarded.

> **For Next Gen:** Before jumping in and telling your new company how bad their site is, consider that it may have been worse! See what any site used to look like by visiting the Wayback Machine, located at https://web.archive.org/. You can find what any website used to look like. This comes in very handy in IP lawsuits!

BUILD FOR MOBILE. BUILD FOR SPEED. BUILD FOR TRAFFIC.

Most agencies know to build for mobile first. It's tempting to build for the big browser screen you are using to review the new work—*but don't do it!!!* Remember, most people will experience your site on their phones. So as you are reviewing design options, pull out your mobile first.

Build for speed. At the time I am typing this, Google is still rewarding and punishing sites based on their loading speeds. There are tests you can perform to see how you rank (this is a favorite sales pitch of digital agencies, I have found!). But this is where the IT side of your team can help with the technical settings to optimize speed.

Build for traffic. If your loading times are sharp, then you can turn your attention to SEO. This is, again, an ever-changing landscape, but the solution seems to be half technical—is everything set so Google can crawl and cache your content?—and half content related. Do the headlines use the keywords that your customers will use? Do you refresh the content on important pages? Do others have links that send traffic to your key pages? Do you have multiple content types on key pages? Text? Images? Videos?

I have found that in midsize companies, there are many content contributors and stakeholders with a shared website.

It is very helpful to have your head of site content do interim updates on what drives good traffic and how it is measured. I can't explain why, but people like to suggest clever or witty headlines. But in the web world, plain speak in keywords wins the day. The first and biggest headline on a page—the H1—should just state what the page is about (e.g., "Best Composite Deck Material for Docks" will work better than "We Know What Floats Your Boat.").

One of the reasons I love digital marketing is that you can see what is working. Each page can be tagged using Google Analytics so you can see how many visits it is receiving, how much of it is organic, and exactly where it's coming from. Not that Google Analytics really needs a plug from me, but it is a powerful tool, and the data can help align stakeholders who are not that close to the web functionality.

ZERO FRICTION, PLEASE

From finding an event date to checking out during an e-commerce transaction, the web experience should be frictionless. Remember the idea of converting hearts and minds? A frictionless experience will give the customer a feeling about your brand, and it helps ensure they convert in the business transaction. In the past, my digital teams have found it useful to run tests in which we assign typical tasks (e.g., buy this kind of item, sign up for this event, find a lung screening test) and then see how easy the task is. The agency measures the time and clicks for a data journey, and then we qualitatively ask them about the experience. We would do this both before and after the refresh.

> **For CEOs:** Even if you are running a not-for-profit, the people visiting your site are also visiting Amazon. They have a certain expectation of how things should work. It's important to remember that and reduce friction for them on all digital touchpoints.

ECOSYSTEM STRATEGY FOR THE MIDSIZE

I recently had a conversation with my friend Ian Gomar, who is a CMO and partner at Chief Outsiders, a fractional CMO firm. Ian reminded me that traditional and digital ecosystems can and will compete with one another if there is not a clear strategy tied to the customer journey and experience. A while back, Ian was working with a prominent women's skincare line. This midsize company sold mostly through category-leading brick-and-mortar retailers and Amazon. They had their own website as well, but it contributed less than 5 percent of their overall business. Given the higher margins on their direct-to-consumer (DTC) website sales, senior management wanted to accelerate growth in this area. The challenge was for management to articulate why a consumer would purchase from their site rather than utilize the convenience of purchasing at a local retail store, or on that retailer's website for the reward points or discounts, or on Amazon, where they'd get free shipping.

"The solution," Ian told me, "was to create a 'reason for being' to shop their website within the brand's ecosystem (which includes traditional and digital channels). The reason we created was driven by current consumer trends of personalization. What if we could create a personalized buying experience for consumers whereby they could create their own skincare regimen tailored to address their needs and issues? And what if that could not be found anywhere else? Well, *that* seemed like the right strategy. Consumers could filter by their skin type and skin issue to create a mix of products that could be purchased as a bundle, even growing into a subscription over time."

So the company pursued a line of skin care products that could be used for different skin types and ailments. Rather than roll out this new line to its retail partners, it managed the opportunity through its DTC site, giving the company the higher revenues it desired, along with a direct link to their customers. Talk about a win-win!

DIGITAL ECOSYSTEMS TO SAVE THE DAY

In March of 2020, most retailers and restaurants closed the doors to their brick-and-mortar establishments. None of us knew how long the shutdown would last or how the pandemic would play out. Almost every retailer and restaurant that could leaned into their digital ecosystems and changed the way they did business. They had to do so in order to survive. I'm sure we all have stories of ordering takeout from our favorite restaurants to ensure they would keep their doors open—and it wasn't just restaurants that had to innovate to stay afloat.

Midsize retailer Crate & Barrel had to close stores for a period of time at the start of the pandemic. Even when stores reopened, they were at limited capacity and hours. Customers shifted to e-commerce, as everyone was more comfortable with ordering online for delivery or curbside pickup.

Before the pandemic, almost all of Crate & Barrel's e-commerce was delivered through their warehouse to the customer. They had a "buy online, pick up in-store" (BOPS) option, but it was more of a pilot program. As online demand soared, the company faced the same capacity constraints as others in the industry. Their warehouse was experiencing record volumes, and they were facing caps from delivery partners. They were concerned they wouldn't be able to meet customers' expectations by only fulfilling online orders through the warehouse. And let's face it: millions of us were fueling the demand by ordering bread makers, kitchen supplies, and furniture to update our homes, where we were dwelling 24/7 during pandemic time.

Digital ecosystem to the rescue. Crate & Barrel quickly enhanced their BOPS experience and rebranded it as "curbside pickup" on their website and across all their communication channels. They implemented software that enabled customers to notify stores when they were on their way or were parked at the curbside location.

The technology team and store operations team partnered to quickly make shipping from stores a reality. They set up additional packing and shipping stations in every store and updated inventory software to allow stores to fulfill overflow orders. Each store location also coordinated the physical curbside staging and delivery process for safety and efficiency.

As a nimble midsize retailer, the company leaned into their digital ecosystem to meet the unanticipated challenge. They repurposed their store network for distribution, fulfilling customer pickups while also shipping nationwide. The pivot resulted in a record-breaking sales year and significant customer growth. I love this success story because even though it is ostensibly about the digital ecosystem and e-commerce, it's really about collaboration and teamwork. Crate & Barrel is a Chicago-based business, and I have friends who participated in this effort. Even as a bystander, I could tell that there was an all-hands-on-deck approach to the solutions that would have made the crew of Apollo 11 proud.

"WHAT WE REALLY NEED IS AN APP"

Unless you are talking about loaded tater tots or calamari, I'm going to challenge you on that one. I mentioned that midsize companies have plenty of enthusiastic stakeholders for big projects. And a common theme I've heard over the last ten years is, "Hey, what we really need is an app!" So I reply with, "Okay, tell me why."

The answers include to be relevant, to build the brand, to get the word out there, "bcz younger people like apps." Only twice have I heard reasons why it would make sense for a user experience and the company's ROI.

This is one of those moments where I turn into the old geezer shouting at the kids to get off my lawn. We don't all need an app. Even though the cost of creating an app has come down, if you are in a midsize company, you need to realize that *building* an app is just the start of the investment. The next step is funding advertising to get people to download the app on their mobile devices, then encourage them to stay engaged. The other essential step is to then update the app for bugs and system upgrades. So if the app itself is central to the business delivery, huzzah! Let's build an app. But otherwise, if the website is optimized for mobile and you are promoting it through multiple digital channels, that may be a better solution.

Remember the legendary Mary Ellen Dugan from the last chapter? She also served as CMO of WP Engine, a company that provides managed hosting solutions specifically for websites, using the popular software WordPress. "When I was at WP Engine," she said, "we spent a lot of time researching how people preferred to engage online since we were a digital experience tech platform. It's no secret that more people, from Gen Zers to baby boomers, are moving to mobile. But the big news story is that people prefer websites versus apps. The website just needs to be mobile responsive and friendly. WP Engine's 'Reality Bytes' study revealed that all generations show a clear preference for a company's website over a mobile app when purchasing online. Baby boomers lead the group, with 85% preferring a website; followed by Gen Xers, with 82% preferring a website; 68% of millennials; and even 61% of Gen Zs.

"This is such an advantage to a company," Mary Ellen continued, "as most will have already invested in a mobile-responsive website. And when customers are searching for your company, they will Google you, looking for a website. Having a mobile-responsive website is so much smarter for SEO and customer experience. And clearly cheaper."

A friend of mine, Pat Dermody, who was the president of an app-based digital-newspaper business told me, "Deciding to load an app on your phone is like deciding to let someone move in with you. It is some precious real estate that you are giving up." Right now, 7 percent of you are still coming up with instances where it may be helpful to have an app for specific goals. And to you I say, "Really think about the return on your investment and time. And get off my lawn!"

TAKEAWAY TRUTHS

1. Start with your website or your primary "conversion machine." Make sure it is optimized before spending money to send customers there.

2. Build for mobile. That does not necessarily mean build an app; it means know that your customer will probably find and work with you from his or her mobile device.

3. Build to be found. With a strong digital ecosystem, it is easier to have a successful SEO strategy and achieve a better return on digital advertising investment.

CHAPTER SEVEN

CONTENT MARKETING:

WORK LIKE A MASTER MATER

What the hell is content marketing, anyhow?

Content can be such a broad variety of things: videos, GIFs, memes, blogs, podcasts, infographics, listicles, quizzes, white papers, case studies, articles, commercials, PSAs, webinars, etc. I recently asked a content director if she could tell me what *isn't* content. My editor has limited me to just one sarcastic comment about the overuse of this buzzword, so I'll stop there.

What I want to share is how to think about content and content marketing in a midsize company with limited budgets and bandwidth.

Let's start with content. Content is anything that would be interesting or educational to your customers. It's the core information and media that's going to populate the website, the app, the newsletter, the YouTube channel, and all the social platforms.

Why is it important? Because brand content is the granular messaging that represents the company's product, brand, and credibility. It can also be the way Google rewards you with organic website traffic through SEO.

You may feel an overwhelming need to produce written and visual "stuff." Like anything, it's best to start with a plan to keep the task sized to the ROI. Without a strategic plan, your team can end up spending excessive time and money.

Here are my first questions when starting to build a strategic content plan:

1. Who produces your content?

2. Do you maximize every opportunity to capture content for a future need?

3. How much do you need?

4. What content is working for customers and your SEO?

WHO PRODUCES YOUR CONTENT?
TO CREATE OR TO CURATE?

The optimal answer will vary by organization, but a good rule of thumb is to tap into your product and customer service teams for content starters. They can provide subject-matter-expert info that may not be ready for primetime consumption but is a great starting point for a marketing team's "zhuzh." Your engineer, public-health specialist, financial analyst, and other subject-matter-expert colleagues can provide the category and product insights that marketing writers and creative teams can convert into articles, infographics, blogs, videos, and testimonials. This can serve as the core of your *create* strategy.

Outside content firms have great value, and they are set up to produce targeted volumes of content at a fairly fast pace. The downside? It can be an expensive habit to keep. I've used content firms to help on targeted campaigns for which we were short-staffed and in areas where we did not have in-house expertise. Content agencies can also be a hybrid solution—a supplemental external newsroom that helps your team on a retainer basis.

Content curation—taking relevant content from other sources and posting it (with credit, of course)—is another option, especially for social media platforms. During the COVID-19 pandemic, the American Lung Association would frequently curate content from the CDC to post on the Lung. org website and publish on our social media platforms. It was highly relevant to our audience and obviated the need to create fresh content that would deliver similar messaging. We often see fashion brands curating looks on Instagram and foodie sites doing the same. For them, curation strategies establish leadership in a category with a side benefit of garnering more followers on a platform.

Ultimately, the marketing team will create a balance of created and curated homegrown and sourced content to fit the overall strategic plan.

Traditionally, content production for a marketing team entails managing the combination of words and images. Copy and graphics. Script and video. You get the picture.

> **For CMOs:** Within the marketing team, content production can potentially be run by different roles, including the CMO. In a small team, it is often helpful to have the head content person be attached to the largest asset that requires content. Who has responsibility for the website, the newsletter, or the primary app? That individual would be a good candidate. Depending on the teams' skill sets, the other choice is your brand director or manager. Whoever it is, I dub them "Keeper of the Word."

Years ago, when I worked at Hallmark Cards, I experienced the ultimate content-coordination-with-a-big-company process. Hallmark had one set of content producers (also known as writers) who wrote the sentiments for greeting cards. They had another group of visual content producers (also known as artists) who created the designs. I was attending my orientation classes with another member of my new-hire cohort, Sari McConnell, when they explained this to us. Then the orientation leader told us the way they paired the artwork with the sentiment was through a specialist called—wait for it—the Master Mater.

No one else in the orientation group batted an eye. Sari and I took one look at each other and burst out laughing until we had to excuse ourselves from the room. We are still friends to this day. She has gone on to run marketing at a midsize music content company and office products companies. And neither of us has ever come across a Master Mater position at a midsize organization.

Video has become such a staple of content for communication that it's worth the investment to have adequate resources. Even with a midsize marketing team, if you can afford a video producer/editor/manager, that is an excellent staffer to have. Ideally, he or she reports to the creative director and can manage freelancers and coordinate with the scriptwriters. Depending on the business, these videos can be highly produced and exact or mobile phone videos dressed up with motion graphics and call-to-action (CTA) end cards.

For Next Gen: Do you have mad TikTok skillz? IG Reels that slay? The most on-point music for your video creations? This can work for you. If you can take your skills and use them for good—or for the brand messaging—you can make an early impact at a midsize.

DO YOU MAXIMIZE EVERY OPPORTUNITY TO CAPTURE CONTENT FOR A FUTURE NEED?

Back in the old days, I would go on commercial shoots. Now I correct my staff if they say "commercial shoot" or "video shoot." It is a content day. With the proper planning, a midsize company can fill its content pipeline by getting more out of these shoots.

The CEO of Real Art Design Group, Chris Wire, told me about a two-day shoot his team had planned for a midsize drinking bottle company. The company had just completed a brand refresh exercise and was ready to move into the development phase with a new sizzle video as a central launch asset. Instead of just filming the scenes on the sizzle video shot list, Real Art also captured multiple product shots and in-use shots with the talent over the course of a couple of days.

In the end, the company was well prepared for the brand relaunch. Not only did they have a compelling new sizzle video, but they also had a boatload of on-brand imagery for the new website and enough owned images for their social media posts and emails to provide fresh content for months.

I've used the same method when creating commercials or PSAs. At AZEK, we had a multiday content shoot across California, capturing beautiful decks and railings at stunning homes. Like Real Art's approach with the drinking bottle company, we captured images and video of product, as well as people and even pets enjoying the beautiful structures. In the end, we had enough for a compelling commercial declaring AZEK's product 100 percent better than wood decks.

We also had a treasure trove of on-brand eye candy for the website, catalogs, emails, and social media posts. We requested that *all* of the video assets from the production company be sent back to the marketing team. That gave us the years-long ability to create re-edits and new video cuts. It makes me smile when I see videos or a commercial from AZEK with some of the footage that we captured on that content shoot years ago.

For CMOs: While content creation is often the "glam" side of the job, keep your company covered with the boring and essential legal details. As shoots move away from the realm of agency-only, it is easy to overlook permission sign-offs for all talent to be used in photos or videos on any of your channels. Ensure this is part of your process and that a particular individual is assigned to tracking it like a bird dog.

HOW MUCH DO YOU NEED?

If your company's product *is* content (yes, I'm looking at you, Morning Brew!), then your needs are off the charts, and this may not apply to you. You may skip ahead.

For the rest of the midsize companies that use content to help market your core service or product, it's helpful to quantify the need for budgeting and staff planning. This should be part of the content strategy plan. My teams have found it most manageable to plan one to three content shoots per year to create owned assets that support product or promotional initiatives. Then we supplement with off-the-shelf imagery from Getty and the like in order to fill the gaps. There are many niche image libraries with a great variety of images that can fit any brand guideline.

Another good way to stretch your created visual content is by using services like Canva. They offer nice-quality designs for social posts and other similar needs. For visual content needs, create your baseline. How many new images do you need for your core channels per month? For your website? Email messages? Social platform posts? Quantify the need, bump it up by 10 percent for the unanticipated opportunities, and then reconcile your budget to the need. This approach will tell you how much you can create, outsource, buy off the shelf, and/or curate.

There is a similar process for written and scripted content, such as podcasts and webinars. Depending on the organization, these needs will vary. For the American Lung Association, website health content and blogs serve many people seeking information. For a while, we were posting two blogs per week, but when our bandwidth was constricted, we ramped down to one per week. To our surprise, there was no drop in overall blog readership. It was an eye-opener to see that when it comes to productivity, more is not always better. Turns out, we could ramp down and refocus those energies.

Creating customer journeys is another great way to determine how much content a company needs. Diet company Noom does a nice job of retargeting consumers with content after they have visited the Noom website or their social posts. Noom has identified multiple motivations a consumer may have for losing weight, and they send emails and create social posts with compelling infographics, insights, and factoids to encourage subscription. I imagine the whiteboards in their offices filled with the content needs to support recruitment, engagement, and evangelism journeys. As a recipient of their emails, I want to say, "I hear you, Noom! I'm just trying to shed that extra COVID-19 weight."

WHAT CONTENT IS WORKING FOR YOUR CUSTOMERS AND YOUR SEO?

When thinking about content, it's important to decide the subject matter and the related keywords where your company should authentically stand out. What should you own? That is where you can prioritize your content efforts.

You can also see what is working for your customers by analyzing their digital response metrics. What gets click-through in your emails? Likes on your social platforms? Which pages and blogs get read on your site? Which video on your YouTube channel exceeds the views of the others? Is it the top topic featuring visual media? These metrics can inform your plan. You can also see how people who consume your content score on your content goals. Do the readers/watchers/listeners do the following?

- Convert into long-term lead generation

- Become new revenue-producing customers

- Become email subscribers

- Stay loyal customers longer

- Become interest groups for retargeting

- Share their stories or become brand evangelists

Some brands use their content instead of advertising because it resonates with their customer base. One of my favorite examples is Pabst Blue Ribbon beer. OMG, my dad used to drink that stuff back in the day. But they put out some hilarious and edgy content on Twitter. They recently created an Easter "Kegg Hunt" around the country and drove traffic to their site for clues. It's not for every brand, but for PBR, their content connects with their loyal and growing "bro" base.

CONTENT AND SEO

Content is one of the *most important* elements of search engine optimization (SEO). It plays a vital role in determining who finds your website and what information they take away once they've landed there. It also plays a vital role in both driving traffic and increasing your conversion rate. While the exact Google SEO algorithms are guarded in a vault next to the secrets of life, Google revealed that they reward content based on how useful, informative, valuable, credible, and engaging it is.

When you think about your content, think about your customers first. What they want to hear should trump what the organization wants to say. SEO is a powerful scorecard, along with the other conversion KPIs mentioned above. But keep it simple and deliver great information on the topics where you should be boss.

CONTENT MARKETING AS A STRATEGY

Using brand content and a content marketing strategy are not exactly the same thing. Branded content can put the business in the spotlight, whereas content marketing is made specifically for an audience's interests.

Content marketing strategy is used to attract, engage, and retain an audience by creating and sharing relevant articles, videos, podcasts, and other media. The focus is on content that is interesting to the *customer* and not directly about the product or services the company is selling. This approach establishes expertise, promotes brand awareness, and keeps your business top of mind when it's time to buy what you sell.

We see many examples of this. REI shares videos, newsletters, etc., on a variety of outdoor or equipment topics. Peloton has an app with free workouts that have nothing to do with the equipment or subscriptions they would like to sell you. Pharma companies will publish white papers, research, and web pages on diseases without promoting the drug they are selling.

> **For CMOs:** Content marketing establishes a company as the credible source on a topic(s), making consumers more likely to refer to them for later purchases. This indirect link to sales or conversion frequently makes this a hard strategy to sell to leadership at a midsize. The secret to success? Don't be such a purist. Create a hybrid content marketing strategy that has some brand or sales conversion points built in. It gives the marketing team some KPIs to test campaign effectiveness.

Marketing has become such a confluence of right-brain and left-brain activity. This is where having the right mix of people on the team is critical. For great content, creative minds will win the day for your brand.

In the next chapter, we'll talk about how the analytical team members will get your content delivered to the right recipients. They will work like Master Maters.

TAKEAWAY TRUTHS

1. Start with a plan for the quantity of content you will need—and decide if you will create it or curate it.

2. Maximize every content opportunity to capture as much for your pipeline as possible.

3. A good content strategy delivers what your customers or potential customers are looking for—not what you are looking to sell.

4. Brand content represents the company's product, brand, and credibility. It can also be the way Google rewards you with organic web traffic through SEO.

CHAPTER EIGHT

DIGITAL ADVERTISING AND SOCIAL MEDIA:

THE LATEST AND GREATEST

When I think about a switch to midsize marketing, I think of Ian Gomar, whom we met in chapter 6. Ian left his position as CMO at Sears Holdings to run Shaquille O'Neal's business ventures and consult for other midsize companies. With a background in CPG and retail, Ian is especially well versed in all elements of digital advertising. When I asked him about the role of digital in a midsize company, he said, "In a midsize, you have to be the person who knows the branding and content *and* know how to get a message out consistently at scale with digital advertising." And then he went on to tell me one of his favorite digital marketing stories:

"I met this company called For Your Party. They sold personalized plates, napkins, and things for weddings. They were vertically integrated, had a reasonable share of the category, and did primarily direct-to-consumer marketing. That is to say, they had their own website, and people found them primarily through SEO, PR, and some paid search and paid social that were underperforming.

"When I met the owner, she said she wanted a plan to grow the business, which had been anemic over the last few years. She pointed out that the people buying wedding party accessories are primarily women twenty-three to thirty years old, and she wondered what a middle-aged, white-haired guy who looked like a US senator with no daughters would know about targeting young women. After much convincing that it wasn't about who I was but rather my marketing experience and ability to change the trajectory of her business, she relented and let me manage her marketing investment and efforts.

"The first step was to replace her marketing agency, which was underperforming and had no idea how to improve. The next step was to eliminate traditional PR, as it was nice to have but showed minimal return on investment, and to reallocate the funds to a higher return on ad spend (ROAS) channel. Within twelve months, we were able to dramatically improve top-line revenue by 30 percent and increase her ROAS from 1.5 to 3.0. Once the paid and organic channels started to improve, we then started to expand and diversify to other potential revenue-generating platforms.

"While researching the category online, we noticed eBay had a lot of wedding and craft products and traffic. So we created some personalized wedding products that were at a higher price point and expanded channels from just DTC to also include eBay and, soon, Amazon.

"At this point, we had increased For Your Party's revenues by double digits, and you would think this is the end of a happy story. But no. COVID-19 hit in spring 2020, and by summer, For Your Party was reeling from the lack of wedding parties. The pandemic literally took their YOY sales down by 75 percent.

"The owner called me back in a panic. What could she do to keep business afloat and avoid layoffs? Then we had the idea: the wedding mask pack. Yes, we customized COVID-19 masks with the names of the bride and groom and the wedding date. They were a huge hit. For Your Party was back in business as we shifted to digitally promote the wedding guest mask packs. The revenue was enough to get the company through the pandemic and into 2022!"

According to Gartner, digital marketing accounts for 85 percent of a CMO's budget. That sounds about right to me. Since roughly 2009, the companies I have worked with have sought me out to advance their digital marketing and transformation. As Ian's story illustrates, this is where new investment is going, and digital continues to produce strong returns. In chapter 6, we covered the conversion machine—the website and digital ecosystem. In chapter 7, we covered the content that advances the organization's goals.

In this chapter, I'd like to share some insights on **how to distribute that content through digital advertising and social media**.

First, this area is highly dynamic, changing every few months. With new privacy regulations and tools like GA4 on the horizon, much will evolve in the near future. So I'll try to stick to the truths as I see them for a midsize and not get lost in the weeds. It's easy to get distracted by all the new digital vehicles and approaches, which is why it's worthwhile to take a step back and connect with the basic marketing funnel.

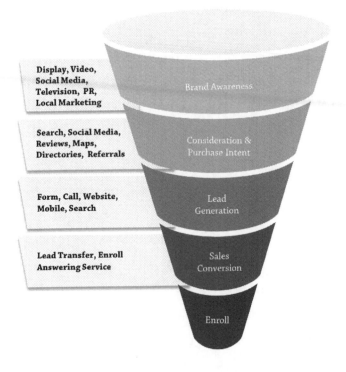

> **For CMOs:** Keep leadership and stakeholders focused on the big picture of content and optimized distribution to hit specific objectives. Digital advertising has no shortage of shiny objects to distract everyone. If I hear "All we need is a TikTok to make this work" one more time . . .

After reconnecting with our old friend, the marketing funnel, the midsize marketing department should focus on the cost per conversion for each channel or tactic. *Conversion* can mean lead generation, purchase, or other end goal. This quick back-of-the-napkin spreadsheet illustrates how to think of the concept. Fortunately, these cost-per-conversion calculations are built into several automated marketing platforms, so they can help with budget allocation. These rubrics are great because as each new opportunity or media pilot is considered, you will have financial context as to how well it needs to perform to earn some of the media budget.

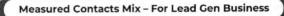

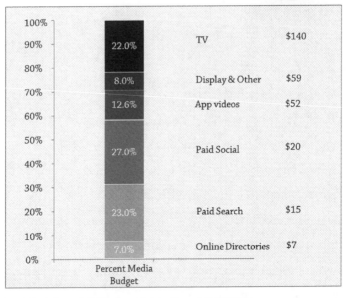

Measured Contacts Mix – For Lead Gen Business

Cost per Contact

Percent Media Budget	Channel	Cost per Contact
22.0%	TV	$140
8.0%	Display & Other	$59
12.6%	App videos	$52
27.0%	Paid Social	$20
23.0%	Paid Search	$15
7.0%	Online Directories	$7

Despite the high attributed cost per contact, TV still drives consumers to the other channels that convert at a lower cost per customer.

The name of the game is budget allocation, and you must pick the right channel and platform to match your audience. I won't bore you with the mechanics or the choices of all the digital channels and products. They are likely to have changed by the time this book is printed anyway. But here are a couple of helpful guideposts for the midsize.

SOCIAL MEDIA

Social media platforms have transformed into advertising platforms. Make sure the leadership team knows it. It's hard to manage expectations if the CEO thinks a product video you post on your FB page is going to "go viral." While it *could,* the odds do not support that. I find it very helpful to be deliberate in conversations about organic social versus paid social.

Organic social posts do not get seen by 100 percent of your social following. A post gets served to 100 percent of your social following if you boost it. (Pay for the privilege.) People who see the organic post without a boost are your loyal followers who Facebook, Instagram, or Twitter think would value seeing your post. Sure, you may have built the social following, but the platform, not your company, "owns" the contacts (shaking my fist in mock rage).

Paid social posts, on the other hand, can go out to just about any target you can describe. Love them or hate them, Facebook still has one of the best returns on ad spending. It is especially helpful to explain this concept to other company stakeholders outside of marketing. Here is a typical exchange I hear from my marketing director:

> Sincere Colleague: Can we advertise this webinar for health-care professionals?
>
> Marketing Director: Sure. What kind of budget do you have?
>
> Sincere Colleague: Ah, I kind of thought we would put it on social media so people could click through and sign up.

Marketing Director: Right. How many people are you expecting, and what's your budget?

Sincere Colleague: I thought we would just put it on our social media page.

Marketing Director: We could, but that will not get you a ton of visibility from the people you want to hit. I don't think it will get the enrollment you want.

Sincere Colleague: Oh. Never mind.

With paid social media, you can use Facebook to target seniors who shop for their pets, Instagram or TikTok to target sorority girls who consume a lot of White Claw, or LinkedIn to target CIOs who manage complex tech stacks. Just make sure the content of your post is compelling, the call to action is clear, and the click-through makes conversion easy.

For CMOs: It may become your job to socialize the concept of paid social media in your company—especially if functional groups need to budget for a specific promotion. The other midsize trap to avoid is trying to be everything to everybody with social media. There are several social media platforms, and you don't have to rock them all. I would suggest prioritizing where you want to shine. Pick the platforms where your core or desired target market spends time. Even though Snapchat still has an impressive user base, it's not the platform where people go to learn more about biomarkers or scientific instruments. Keep the choices customer-centric.

Remember, if you are posting on a regular basis, customers should be responding to you. So for all your platforms, you need someone who is going to handle community management. It's plausible that your staffer who is creating and posting for you could do community management—but depending on the volume and tenor of the feedback, it can become overwhelming for one person.

At the American Lung Association, we had one person handling our national social media, and whenever we would run a campaign to stop youth vaping, the Big Tobacco trolls would show up. They posted such venomous statements and contorted untruths that it took a toll on the social media manager. Sure, she could hide or delete their nasty posts but not before she read them. A steady diet of toxic community management guarantees turnover. I learned that the hard way.

> **For Next Gen:** Community management is an incredibly important role. It's literally the company's front line, where you get product ideas, brand love, great questions, and sometimes very negative energy. Make sure you are trained on response procedures, and even then, if negativity gets stressful, let your supervisor and team members know. You have to look out for your own vibes.

Today, using Influencers as part of any company's marketing mix is as fundamental a priority as TV advertising was for brands in the '90s. Consumers believe and convert far more quickly when they hear about a brand from a source they trust, "know," and follow on social networks. That being said, influencers range from everyday loyal followers on your own brand's social platforms to paid celebrities talking about your brand and many varieties in between.

Influencers are classified by how many Followers they have on their own social networks. When they are engaged with your brand, they post creative messages on their networks, which reach their audiences and amplify brand awareness:

- Nano/Micro (everyday loyal Followers)
- Mid-Tier (50–500k Followers)
- Macro (500k–1 million Followers)
- Mega and Celebrity (1 million+ Followers)

You can start building a Nano/Micro network by employing a community manager who will create regular dialogue with your own social media Followers, then give the most loyal of them free products or gifts to tell their social networks about your brand. This is often called a Brand Ambassador program.

The best Mid-Tier, Macro, and Mega Influencers are people who use your product and may have reached out to tell you they like it. They are paid spokespeople who are usually used to support a specific campaign, delivering a message you've asked them to share. They message about your product on their social networks to spread the news to thousands of their Followers. You do not dictate what specifically they will show or say because each has their own style, but they will follow the business objectives and guidelines you provide.

You can also source Influencers from firms that represent influencers of all types. You can find influencers who talk about retirement funds or nurses who talk about asthma. Aspire Brands, for example, uses an array of ambassadors and influencers to drive awareness and consideration. "We've had some strong success with mid-tier and nano influencers who have authentic voices that match with our brand," says CMO/CSO Kim Feil. "Aspire wants to celebrate some Aspirational women, specifically professional women athletes and professional women—especially nurses—who could use an even amount of energy all shift or all day. We recently partnered with athletes from the National Women's Soccer League and women pro golfers, and their authentic use and affinity to the brand has been a great match."

That said: it isn't all sunshine and Instagram likes. It can be challenging to measure the business results beyond the awareness Influencers generate with their networks. Kim feels the influencer industry is having a boom right now, but performance measurement will become more rigorous. "There are a lot of influencers out there who just do the 'product grab and grin' social posting," she says, "and it's not differentiated or inspiring. With a product called Aspire, I would hope that they could share the product with a relevant aspirational story, but it doesn't always work out that way."

Moral of the story: influencers are very important in your marketing mix; just look for authentic connections that support your brand in a relevant way.

EMAIL MARKETING

When we go back to the basics of choosing the lowest cost per conversion channel, I'm going to bet that most of our companies will have SEO and email as the most economical choices. If you have someone's email address in your database, you have some tangible connection with that individual. Email is almost always the #1 ROI channel.

Email can be used to maintain customer engagement or convert them to buy at key times or with specific offers. There is also a lot of work maintaining the data, pulling in as much appended data as possible about these customers, and hitting the right balance with messaging cadence. This is an art and science balance of content and delivery.

Regardless of your midsize business model, B2B, B2C, or some combo of these, I recommend an email marketing service or a marketing automation platform to help with this work. The ability to segment lists, send at the best time of day, and suppress addresses gets too big to handle with spreadsheets. A platform can also help with repetitive touchpoints such as win-back programs, welcome series, and any other specific customer journeys and drip campaigns.

There are so many choices of platforms. And once you start to research them online, they will hound your inbox incessantly. Most promise some variety of marketing automation, email automation, personalization, and analytical functionality. Most handle the tasks I listed in the paragraph above. Many also offer some sort of AI or machine-learning feature as well.

As a midsize, you may consider an email marketing service such as Constant Contact, Sendinblue, Moosend, EmailOctopus, or Mailchimp. They all have good features, and they integrate with your other services. But it will be up to your team to always manage the data integrations as your other tools update or change.

The other route is an automated marketing platform, such as Salesforce Marketing Cloud, Pardot, Marketo, or HubSpot. They are bigger and more expensive but are built as a platform to integrate across all of your customer channels and customer journeys. The automated marketing platforms are a commitment, and life is easier if you have staff who have worked in them before and are not simply learning as they go. Everyone can take "trailhead classes" and still not know how to put the whole end-to-end opportunity together.

> **For CMOs:** Spending the time to find the right platform is important. It's also just the beginning of a multi-month process. It takes a team time to get trained in a new platform and to get all of the data flows optimized. If you have more tools connecting to the automated platform (Shopify, Gravity Forms, WordPress, etc.), it will take longer for your team to confidently rock it. Have a realistic time frame to stand up a new automated marketing platform and to master its use.

DIGITAL ADVERTISING

Moving down the conversion chart, we find the paid digital advertising options. This is really where an optimized balance of awareness-driving, engagement, and conversion comes into play. There are more precise how-to books and conferences on digital marketing details, so I'll assume you already know a little about this topic and stick to what to manage as a midsize.

Search. Of the paid digital options, search—and specifically branded search—will be the best ROI option. It makes intuitive sense, right? Someone self-identifies as interested in your brand or the keyword by typing it into Google. They are already down the funnel, and you just have to make sure they don't get distracted by another advertiser or that you don't lose them with a bad conversion experience once they click through the search ad.

There is an ongoing question about whether you should buy your own branded terms or hope that the person ends up on your website through SEO since they are already typing your brand name. I generally buy the branded search terms as they are the best-performing ROI terms. To be certain of their value, every so often, back off of buying them to quantify the impact. Then decide.

Usually, branded search terms increase in tandem with other top-of-the-funnel advertising. If you advertise on television, you will see the corresponding bump in your branded search activity. People see a message on their bigger screen and then interact on their phone or laptop. You win!

For CEOs: If you think people who type in your brand name are going to convert without your company's investing any money, you may have it wrong. If your brand is a leader in your category, smaller brands will buy your brand name in an effort to hijack customers who were looking for you.

Buying a competitor's brand as a search term is a totally legitimate practice. However, Google will shut down advertisers if they go so far as to misrepresent themselves as another company. I've been on both sides of this competitive keyword play. At Sylvan, when we were investing in TV advertising, smaller tutoring firms would buy our name so they could show up and potentially get a click when viewers were responding to our commercials. It used to burn me up. They were drafting on our media investment! However, when I was working at a company that was *not* the market share leader, I tried buying the category leader's brand name, expecting to score big. The results? We had a reasonable number of click-throughs, but the cost per click was so much higher than my branded or category keywords that we soon dropped the strategy.

DISPLAY

We already covered the next most productive channel, which is paid social. So the next channel for most organizations to consider is display. Display helps get a message out and can produce some click-throughs, but it's not a great conversion vehicle. That does not mean it's not valuable. Since you are midsize, you'll want an agency partner who can execute programmatic buys for you. They will blend retargeting, lookalike targeting, and behavioral retargeting to try to get your ads in front of the audience most likely to eventually convert.

Video advertising is another high-engagement form of display advertising. This is great for engagement, especially on YouTube. Again, these formats do not usually show great direct ROI, but attribution models reveal they are a frequent start of the consumer journey to convert. They're also fantastic ways to get your brand or product message to the right audience.

CONNECTED TV (CTV)

I love this newish channel. For the midsize company, it's an opportunity to have a TV commercial and the follow-up digital ads to encourage conversion. I always used to preach, "We are living in the era of two screens: the big one on your customer's wall and the small one in her hand. You have to invest in both." Yeah, well, that is old-school now. CTV has blended these worlds.

Connected TV combines the impact and prestige of TV with optimization, attribution, and targeting at a large scale. It's a perfect combination of the experience of television and the precision of digital advertising. CTV ads are shown only on large screens (via smart TVs, Hulu, Roku, etc.) and on blue-chip TV networks (NBC, HGTV, ESPN, and the like). CTV ads are highly targeted to first-party audiences and third-party audience data from Oracle. After a user sees a CTV ad on his or her large screen, all devices (including phones and tablets) associated with that household are shown banner ads through IP address retargeting. The ads are activated through a performance-based platform with the ability to follow users to the point of conversion.

Ali Haeri, vice president of marketing at MNTN—a leader in the CTV space—shared his thoughts on what CTV means for marketers in the midsize space: "Digital options such as CTV allow midsize companies and brands to take advantage of awareness-driving tactics like television in a way they previously could not have afforded. It also gives them the ability to target their message, send follow-up messages to their target audience, and measure the effectiveness of their campaigns. It's a great vehicle for these organizations that need to get the most out of every marketing dollar."

> **For CMOs:** Have I already mentioned digital advertising is a dynamic arena? It's true. And you will have stakeholders with different levels of understanding regarding how the digital platforms work. One of my biggest challenges is finding the right level of detail for the right audience (my peers, my boss, the board). You want to invite people to understand, ask good questions, and become comfortable, but pulling a meeting down a rabbit hole is a common hazard with this topic.

Get a highly digital staffer and a digital media agency that's a good fit for a midsize. They will steer you through a whole lot of "new" that is coming at us marketers. With new privacy rules, the cookie-less internet, and who knows what else in the metaverse, even as I write this, I am reminded every day of how much new stuff I don't know.

TAKEAWAY TRUTHS

1. Don't get lost in all the new digital options. Understand what you need from the marketing funnel and choose the channels that serve that need.

2. Keep your eye on cost per acquisition. As CPMs rise, your digital media mix may shift.

3. Email is not dead. It's still a high-ROI channel and an excellent part of your omnichannel strategy.

4. Remember that digital advertising is the vehicle to connect content with the right customer and lead them to a frictionless conversion. Digital advertising is not the end goal; it is the medium.

CHAPTER NINE

TIMING IS EVERYTHING:

MIND THE CALENDAR
AND YOUR MONEY

"With my mind on my money and my money on my mind."

—Snoop Dogg

I f you are working at a midsize, you can't afford to waste money or time.

When I was working at a private equity portfolio company as a CMO, we were trying to dial in the digital advertising to optimize lead generation for the franchisees. I was trying to make the process move faster than it would at a normal, comfortable pace, and I was clearly irritating my CTO colleague.

He looked at me and said, "I get what you are trying to do. But really, what's the rush?"

Did I mention it was a private equity company that had a clear sell date for us? I was seriously taken aback by his question; I couldn't fathom how he didn't feel the urgency.

THE THING ABOUT TIME

Know how time works for your company. For a midsize, it's critical to manage the calendar, ensuring planning time to support good execution. In toy manufacturing, we would meet in Hong Kong in the summer to finalize the next year's line. We would get prototypes and samples in September and present them to the major retailers at the October toy show or at their offices. Based on their reaction, we would start creating commercials for key items in the fall. In February, at Toy Fair, we would show retailers the packaging, product, and the advertising plan. Then they would decide how much volume to order. In spring, our factories would manufacture the toys, and the product was on the boat coming to the US from June through August. Retailers would set their aisles in September, and we would run promotional campaigns for the "hard eight" weeks up until Christmas. No surprises.

Every business has a cycle like that. When you know those key moments in which your customer is open to buy, you have to design everything around it—or wait for your next opportunity. With toys, that opportunity comes a year later.

Kim Feil offered some insight into the "health and lifestyle" cycle that is crucial for Aspire Brands. "We are in Q2 of the current year, and I was just discussing industry timing with our head of sales. We want to launch a big campaign and expand a customer in Q1 next year. But to prepare this effectively and devote resources to making a Q1 impact, we have to let go of some smaller Q4 opportunities that would otherwise distract this effort. It requires a lot of discipline, but we agree that for a health drink, industry timing points to 'new year, new habits' as the big opportunity. If we are going to be on time for the biggest opportunity, in a business-changing way, we need to prioritize."

If you realize your marketing deliverables are out of sync with your organization's key customer moments, one solution is to skip less critical activity for a couple of months. Granted, this feels like anathema to a midsize company. But at some point, you have to say, "All right; we're not going to chase anything new for these two months so that in June, we have our shit together." That is a hard pill to swallow, but sometimes it's the only way to get ahead of the curve so that you can be aligned with the business cycle and key deliverables. Timing is everything, and it's useless to have a perfect pitch or campaign if you show up after the window of opportunity has closed.

"In a growing midsize, it is hard to be planful," Kim said. "It just is. There are so many urgent opportunities and tasks that it can be difficult to plan ahead to hit future goals in a big way. Meeting the immediate demand becomes job one, but making sure big ideas happen takes advanced planning, and optimizing the industry cycle requires discipline."

For CEOs: From your viewpoint, what is out of sync with the organization's core delivery cycle? Product development? Marketing decks? Supporting financials? If it is marketing, can you facilitate what your CMO can *stop* doing to get the critical work back in sync with the priority needs?

Professor Harry M. Jansen Kraemer Jr. from the Kellogg School of Management writes about the concept of time in his book *Your 168: Finding Purpose and Satisfaction in a Values-Based Life.* For you math whizzes: you will have guessed that 168 is the total of twenty-four hours times seven days a week. In this book, he challenges us as individuals and as leaders to be truly mindful and reflective of how we spend our time. For instance, when you are managing your personal week or organizational week, you can't keep adding tasks without also dropping some.

I find this to be a powerful concept when planning how to get my marketing teams in sync with the greatest organizational needs. Professor Kraemer is also a master at pointing out the noncritical things that so many of us do that consume our 168 without our accomplishing what we say is important. He affords us all the grace of being human and taking each tomorrow as a time to recommit ourselves to our priorities. He also shares his two guiding rules for himself that I have found so useful: 1) Do the right thing and 2) Do the very best you can.

INTEGRATED MARKETING: GETTING AS MUCH OUT OF YOUR TIME AS POSSIBLE

The CMO has more control over another key timing issue: optimizing campaigns with integrated marketing. The concept is simple: several messaging activations run concurrently for a larger impact. If the email that goes out to your database looks like the post that's on your social media, which looks like the ads you're running on CTV, and indeed they all say the same thing, you are more likely to get your message through to your customer—and in a shorter period of time. Duh.

But it's surprising how many organizations don't take the time to have staff coordinate with each other to integrate channels and content. If you do not reinforce each channel's communication, you are wasting time and money by diluting the campaign's impact. It takes intentional discipline, planning, and coordination to make marketing integration part of the team's DNA. New project management tools and automated marketing platforms have made it easier for a midsize company to consistently integrate marketing channels.

For CMOs: Putting the marketing and content calendar together during yearly planning is the special sauce for keeping your team ahead of the clock. It gives you time to coordinate national and local efforts, time to innovate, time to create great content, and time to make something worthy of your customer.

THE THING ABOUT MONEY

While there are so many rewards to working in a midsize, there are some larger risks as well. Specifically, money. It is easy for things to get really bad, really quickly, when working with a revenue and profit base smaller than those of a large corporation.

If there is strong organizational leadership, financial ruin is rarely on the horizon. However, the pandemic's toll on multiple business sectors was a primer in financial vulnerability. Larger companies were in a consistently better position to sustain the economic impact of the business disruption. When I returned to work in downtown Chicago, I found that my go-to Dunkin' and Protein Bar had survived. (All glory given!) But unfortunately, many of the independently owned restaurants and bars did not.

The secrets to managing financial risk as a midsize marketer? Be fiscally conservative, be transparent with the finance team, and spend money as if it were your own.

Depending on the business, the marketing department can easily represent one of the big investment areas in the organization's budget. Content creation and media investments, events, PR, and collateral can add up quickly. So what is an appropriate budget? And how does a marketing team pivot if sales go unexpectedly up or down?

At the beginning of the year, having a target advertising-to-sales (A:S) ratio is helpful. This should be established with the leadership team based on past sales and marketing investment analytics. Then, if there is an unanticipated drop in revenue, marketing has guidance on how to adjust spending down to the new revenue forecast. This helps to manage the impact on profit.

According to my tech CMO friends, within the SaaS and tech subscription business models, instead of a sales or top-line revenue number, they tend to use annual recurring revenue (ARR). This is roughly the amount of revenue from newly acquired customers, plus the predictable amount from current or renewing customers minus the churn from departing customers. To plan for marketing budgets in these markets, there is usually a percentage of ARR. That percentage can vary broadly depending on how big of a role marketing plays and how closely marketing impact is tied to sales.

> **For Next Gen:** Understand the ratio of marketing spend to revenue growth. You don't want to spend money just for the sake of "doing stuff." Sometimes keeping the money in the bank is the smarter move.

Today, marketing budgets are generally more fungible than those of other departments. Not so long ago. More channels— TV, print, OOH—had longer planning horizons and contracts that were inflexible expenses. Now, with digital advertising, there are fewer media commitments that can't be canceled with just a couple of weeks' lead time. So even if the marketing budget is a hefty line item on the org budget, it can be cut as the year progresses and the financial forecast becomes clear. Conversely, if there is a channel that is delivering impressive ROI, you should invest beyond the original budget.

> **For CMOs:** Don't be a whiner. If your budget gets a haircut or gets blown up in service of the bottom line, celebrate the fact that your badass planning allowed the flexibility the organization needed. At the C-suite level, you are probably compensated on org profit, not the cool factor of the ill-fated brand campaign you just graciously canned. In the words of Kim Feil, "Be ready to adapt your scope to a changing reality. Know when you have to flex up or down."

SHINY OBJECTS

Possibly more than any other organizational department, marketing gets tempted by shiny new objects. They come in the form of consultants offering an analytics audit, new social platform advertising, an acquisition campaign, a TikTok campaign, automated marketing systems, creative agencies, cause marketing, upgraded martech stacks, etc., etc., etc. Some of these new ideas will help you reach the company's stated goals. Some will not. For most of them, you don't *really* know the ROI from the start.

I've chased a few of these over the years with varying degrees of success and failure. I have three strategies for managing the financial impact of shiny objects:

1. Ask the vendor hard questions, such as how they can help you hedge the risk of investing with them.

2. Consider trying a pilot before committing to a serious investment.

3. Talk to others about their performance. The new vendor will give you references but do the work of asking other networks about their track records.

If you are considering a large investment, you want to mitigate the risk to the best of your ability.

Next Gen: Before you get on the cheer squad for a new shiny object, take a moment. How would the CEO regard the opportunity? Be brutally honest with yourself. Would this new initiative help the company make more money? Is it worth the team's valuable time? Be judicious and then voice your opinion.

If you are working in a midsize, there are two things you can't afford to waste: money and time.

 TAKEAWAY TRUTHS

1. Take a critical look at the seasonal cycles in your industry. Is your marketing in sync? If you are showing up two weeks or two months late, it's a problem you can fix.

2. It's important for a midsize to integrate marketing channels to get the most impact from campaign investments and time.

3. Be fiscally responsible. No marketer has ever regretted this strategy. This includes being judicious about funding the new shiny objects.

CHAPTER TEN

KPIs & REPORTING:

THOSE SEXY MONSTERS

KPIs (Key Performance Indicators) get a bad rap as boring follow-up work. Not every marketer sees them as the sexy monsters they are. In truth, if you can't measure the marketing's impact, it is very difficult to justify funding it. Conversely, **clear, consistent KPIs can prove out the value of channels** such as social media and CTV to win over internal skeptics.

The old adage is, "What gets measured gets managed." The key marketing impact numbers are different for every company. New product sales, leads, e-commerce revenue, site traffic, conversions, email database growth, loyalty members, share of voice, brand awareness, new customers, repeat customers, and project tickets are just some of the usual numbers that get tracked.

I have also found that setting up the KPIs at the beginning of a project or campaign ensures that all of the stakeholders are aligned. It forces you to ask questions like, "What is the most important outcome: acquisition or purchase?" The answer will impact the content, the media approach, and then the KPI.

> **For CEOs:** Ask your CMO to front-load the KPIs that are most important to you and that impact the other functional areas in the monthly reporting. And read the report.

KNOW YOUR AUDIENCE

I've been told that marketers, as a group, can be prone to over-sharing. I fell into this trap in my early days at a private equity portfolio company with quarterly board reports. My CFO was very helpful when he pointed out that the board only needs to see three to five numbers from marketing and that while my 17+ KPIs may be very precious to me, they are not needed for that audience. In fact, he pointed out if I publish numbers that are not related to the key business drivers and investments, I risk creating futile, time-consuming conversations that waste valuable focus time with the board. That was excellent advice that I continue to keep with me.

For CMOs: I was very fortunate to have a CFO partner who gave me honest feedback. When preparing to deliver KPIs or reports to a board or new group, find a coach within the set of team members who can give candid guidance on the best level of information to include. #PreventOvershare

The leadership team may want a KPI report that's a little more detailed—especially if some of the numbers are tied to performance in other functional areas. A prime example is that my sales partners are always interested in lead generation metrics and email file growth. I have found it most useful to deliver a monthly KPI report in a consistent format with YOY growth data.

This serves a couple of purposes in a midsize company. First, it reminds your staff what is important and being measured. Second, it gives your CEO and C-suite colleagues insight into marketing metrics that drive the business. Third, and perhaps most important, shared reporting drives a spirit of transparency and co-accountability in all the functional areas. Remember, the report goes out when there is good news as well as when there is bad news.

Kristen Simmons is a marketing and management executive with deep expertise in consumer experience. She currently serves as chief operating officer at PeopleConnect. When we were discussing the role of KPIs in midsize companies, she immediately recalled an experience at a Southern California healthcare company where she had worked.

"We launched a consumer experience (CX) survey to get a baseline net promoter score (NPS), as well as other useful insights from our customers. To me, these seemed like mandatory CX data that any company would need. However, when we shared the planned initiative with the executive leadership team, the CFO questioned whether the value of the output would justify the time invested. Would this information really enable smarter decisions and drive more business?

"The CX team worked hard to ensure readouts were customized and actionable for each internal audience, but we took nothing for granted. As folks who prided ourselves on useful research, we extended this philosophy to our internal customers. We launched a brief, anonymous survey that asked staff directors across the company, 'Can you identify a smarter business decision you've made in the past six months as a result of having these customer insights?' The response to that survey was overwhelmingly positive; over 80 percent said yes. So we had internal-usage KPIs on the relevance of our customer-facing KPIs!

"Cross-functionally, everyone was convinced of the CX survey's value. Seeing the internal data made a big difference to our CX team too, energizing them with a reinforced sense of purpose."

> **For CEOs:** If you have service centers in your organization, and their customers are other internal groups, they should still have performance KPIs! Those internal metrics keep everyone honest about what is working and what is not.

WHAT KPIS DO THE MARKETING TEAM NEED?

The KPIs should tie back to the team members' performance objectives. So the monthly reporting should eliminate any surprises at year-end evaluation time. The digital staffers will use the metrics on a weekly basis to adjust everything from keywords promotion to paid social and advertising allocations. For the marketing team as a whole, the KPIs should help with the productivity analysis of content and channels. At any point in time, they should tell you what your highest productivity channel is, along with your lowest.

Now *that* is hot.

> **For CMOs:** Always be ready with data to answer the following question: "If I gave you an extra $100,000 to spend, where would you spend it?" The answer should be based on ROI numbers or projected returns if it is invested in infrastructure or people. Conversely, always be ready with a data-based answer if the question is this: "What would you cut if the budget were reduced by 20 percent?"

Another useful KPI for the CMO is internal activity measurement. For staff who receive requests from internal partners, tracking KPIs helps quantify the work volume.

One example is a graphics team's workload. In my current organization, the small graphics group receives work requests from a broad range of internal staffers through a ticketing system. When our creative director told me he thought they were becoming overwhelmed by the workload, I had to ask him to quantify that for me. At first, he was not sure how to respond. He had been using the ticketing system to ensure work was tracked and completed, but he had not used it to chart overall workloads.

Once he pulled a historical activity report, it was easy to understand the rising number of tickets per month and the need for other resources to prevent workflow bottlenecks. It was also easy to share the data with the leadership team for buy-in. They could see that their teams would be impacted if there was an inadequate number of graphics people to handle the workflow.

In a midsize organization, these KPIs are helpful to stay ahead of resource shortages and to keep payroll decisions tied to metrics.

LET THOSE SEXY KPIS SHINE

How the data is presented can make a big difference. Data visualization is the best way to quickly communicate information and make a clear point. While most larger companies have business intelligence (BI) or analytics teams to produce awe-inspiring charts and dashboards, I posit that a midsize marketing department can do a respectable job.

Northwestern professor Steve Franconeri tells us that over 40 percent of our brains are dedicated to visual comprehension. So your audience is prewired to comprehend an infographic or chart. He adds that the biggest caution is to make sure your audience is perceiving the same takeaway point you intended to make, as charts and data visualizations can tell multiple stories. Using colors, callouts, and commentary, you can bring your data story to life.

Take, for example, the data visualization below. Let's say you're given a simple task: to find the highest values. Now compare the two tables side by side. See how easy it is to find the highest values *with* color coding? It's almost impossible to find them without it.

Data Visualizations work because your visual system is so powerful

72	50	64	18	23	47	48	67
64	87	61	18	40	64	88	15
17	31	78	41	56	87	42	33
63	37	59	15	11	55	30	63
55	48	49	22	22	56	66	61
48	21	79	34	45	84	57	50
21	94	54	12	28	20	94	19
80	37	50	64	54	31	38	74

There are several data-visualization software options to help with dashboards and charts. Tableau is the big name, though Domo, Adverity, and others can make your marketing team look very polished. But even the chart function in Microsoft Office can do the job. A secret to helping data presentations is that the brain center that processes your written bullet points (reading) is the same area that processes language. So your audience cannot read your slide and listen to you talk at the same time. However, they *can* simultaneously absorb an image and listen to you speak. Brilliant, right? So bring on the infographics!

To illustrate just how powerful this concept is, I have to share a story: Chris, a screenwriter friend of mine, was presenting a slideshow of his TV pilot to a roomful of Hollywood executives. The execs literally said to him, "We don't get it. Can you make this presentation without words?" Once he swapped out the text for pictures, they bought the pilot.

Are you seeing the big picture? Use pictures, not words!

> **For Next Gen:** Were you asked to publish the KPIs for the campaign? The monthly marketing metrics? Don't view it as grunt work. This is a chance to hone your data visualization and get your mad skillz recognized. Communicating data clearly will be a skill that will always serve you.

KPIS FOR CONTEXT

When I first joined the American Lung Association, the members of the board would frequently say, "We love what the Lung Association does, but it seems like we are the country's best-kept secret. No one sees what we do." I took this very seriously and started my first thirty-day activity by monitoring the organization's presence in media and on social media.

What was startling to me is how frequently we were in the news across the country. It was far from a problem; I'd have classified our media presence as an asset. We were getting coverage in local and national publications on a variety of lung-health topics. But this level of coverage would not be evident to individual board members unless they had their Google Alerts so finely tuned as to catch us in all the sources we appeared. The big question was this: Which KPI would give them a sense of transparency and progress regarding the organization's visibility?

What they really needed was context for the American Lung Association's presence. Just seeing the number of news stories or the number of impressions would not be especially helpful. My comms team worked with Cision and pulled together data on how frequently the American Lung Association showed up in the news on four key topics: lung cancer, youth vaping, clean air, and COVID-19. Then they combined that data with that of the other public health organizations that were involved in the same subject areas. This allowed us to show our share of voice (SoV) to the board in a way that made sense to them. They could see that we were easily #1 or #2 in the areas that meant most to us that year.

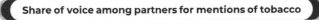

Share of voice among partners for mentions of tobacco

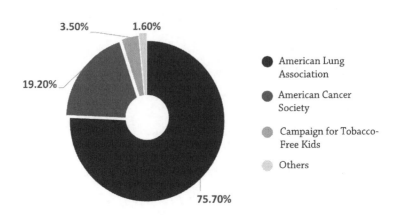

3.50%   1.60%

19.20%

75.70%

- American Lung Association
- American Cancer Society
- Campaign for Tobacco-Free Kids
- Others

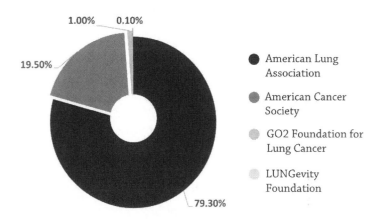

Share of voice among partners for mentions of lung cancer

1.00% 0.10%
19.50%
79.30%

- American Lung Association
- American Cancer Society
- GO2 Foundation for Lung Cancer
- LUNGevity Foundation

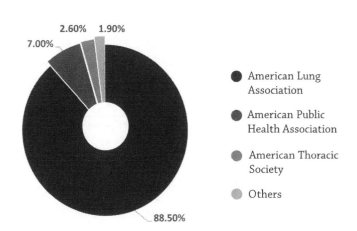

Share of voice among partners for stories mentioning healthy air

2.60% 1.90%
7.00%
88.50%

- American Lung Association
- American Public Health Association
- American Thoracic Society
- Others

Reporting and KPIs are great explainers and scorecards. If you are in a midsize and are staying agile, they become the road signs showing what is working and what is not. Now how is that not sexy?

TAKEAWAY TRUTHS

1. KPIs clearly track what marketing is doing for the midsize. They can serve as both motivators and caution signs.

2. Great data visualization can help more stakeholders understand your point in less time.

3. Reporting and KPIs can help set context, dispel myths, and encourage data-informed decisions.

CHAPTER ELEVEN

THE FUTURE OF MIDSIZE MARKETING:

THE MAGIC 8 BALL SAYS . . .

People often ask me what the future of marketing or midsize marketing looks like. While I do not have a crystal ball, there are a few trends that, in my opinion, will shape how we'll work in the future.

I wrote this book at a moment in time when many people are reevaluating where and how they are working. Millions of people quit their jobs in 2021 and 2022 to find something that was a better personal fit or offered better compensation. Popular media today calls this the "Great Resignation," a byproduct of the pandemic. The accepted wisdom is that after the big COVID-19 shift of working from home, not working at all, or working from anywhere, people started to question how they wanted to work. This, in turn, has created a labor shortage.

But let's get real. The labor shortage started before the pandemic, and COVID-19 just accelerated it. To look at the future of midsize marketing, we must look at the state of consumers and the people who would join the marketing team ranks today. The labor shortage is a trend that will impact the future of marketing and all business.

There are fewer people coming into the workforce, as the birth rate in the US flattened in 2008 and has been declining since 2014. We just saw the first uptick in 2021 as the COVID-19 babies bumped up the rate. Birth rates have declined at even steeper rates in other countries, and the reality is that there will be fewer new workers available in much of the world. With COVID-19, more older workers decided to retire early, further diminishing the size of the workforce. So **one of the obvious future trends has to be automation of work that is repetitive and replaceable.** With fewer workers, we will want to be deliberate about where humans add value and where automation can help. Think how this could play out with customer service, events, merchandising, shooting TV commercials, and more.

The other future trend will be the use of AI to augment the workforce. Checkers Drive-In Restaurants, a midsize quick-service restaurant chain, brought in excellent AI software to help take drive-through orders so their staff could have more eye contact and human connection with the customer at the key moment. The AI accuracy rate was excellent, and it relieved some of the time-pressure stress from workers in the restaurants that were running short-staffed during the pandemic.

So many aspects of marketing will be augmented by AI, ranging from media algorithms to content creation. The language-processing AI is so sophisticated now that in the near future, many communication tasks will be delegated to software. Today, Generative Pre-trained Transformer 3 (GPT-3) is a deep-learning autoregressive large-language model using 175 billion parameters—and it's now open for public use. It has the ability to create humanlike copy, songs, and stories. Other tech firms, including Microsoft, Nvidia, and Google, are developing even more advanced AI language models and expanding the marketing use possibilities.

While video is the pervasive media format now, midsize marketers will need to level up to leverage the metaverse with AR and VR. I'm not going to bet the bank on consumers all adopting big goggles, but gaming, virtual meeting rooms, scale models of everything from houses to communities, and more will all be available. Imagine thinking of metaverse settings as advertising platforms. If a consumer finds himself strolling through a virtual world, will he see a certain brand of sunglasses or a specific kind of car as a product placement? Citibank estimates that the metaverse economy will be worth $13 trillion by 2030, with five billion global users.

The martech stack will continue to be important as we eventually drop the buzzword "digital transformation" and just say "business." The ability to easily access customer data so brands can address individuals as individuals will become table stakes in marketing departments. Today, midsize companies are still wrestling with the adoption of marketing automation platforms to get to customer personalization. But the platforms will have to evolve so that any midsize can get the right messaging and channels synchronized for a seamless customer journey.

Midsize companies will also realize that digital transformation has less to do with the tech tools and more to do with a culture that embraces data and adapts work processes. There is an excellent podcast in Brené Brown's *Dare to Lead* series in which she interviews Harvard Business School's professor Linda Hill. Professor Hill gives an insightful look into the role of culture and leadership in the talk titled "Leading with Purpose in the Digital Age." It is an excellent primer for preparing a midsize marketing department for the future.

The marketing team will probably have different titles in the near future as well. We will lose the hard separation between traditional marketing and digital marketing. There will only be *marketing*. Tasks and titles will probably reflect content creation and channel delivery instead of branding versus digital. I'm also assuming that the chief digital officer and the chief marketing officer will be the same person. No, they won't become a hybrid person like your favorite science-fiction hero. They will still be human, just wearing two hats.

COVID-19 has also opened our eyes to some changes that will shape the future long past the pandemic. One that comes to mind is shooting and production for content and commercials. In August of 2020, the American Lung Association was supposed to shoot our PSAs for youth vaping prevention. The challenge was finding a way to keep the actors, director, and production staff safe at a time when we did not yet have vaccines. We were working with the Ad Council and Hill Holliday, and they came up with a brilliant solution. They rewrote the PSA spots so that the actors would deliver minimal lines while looking straight at the camera and then the rest of the messaging would be delivered in the form of on-screen copy. The production company delivered the backdrop, laptops, and camera to three actors' homes and helped them set up the lighting and camera via Zoom calls. Then the director worked with them via Zoom to get the footage for the PSA. Hill Holliday set my team up in a virtual greenroom where we could watch the filming and approve everything.

In the end, the PSAs urging parents to "get their heads out of the clouds" about vaping were powerful, effective, and inexpensive. Even this year, when we are all vaccinated and boosted and the production company could shoot live, my team participated from a virtual greenroom, saving thousands of dollars in time and travel. We can make amazing creative content without all the legacy costs, and *that* will shape future budgets and planning.

THE PACE OF CHANGE: MARKETING WILL BE THE NARRATOR

The pace of change in the last fifty years has been mind-blowing. With everything from the evolution of the internet to mobile computers we all carry with us (a.k.a. phones) to the fact that we developed a vaccine for a pandemic and inoculated much of the world in a two-year time frame, the speed of change has been remarkable. And with technology, global collaboration, and available capital, we should anticipate even more change in the next ten years.

What does that have to do with marketing? Everything! Marketing will narrate the changes and position them so consumers can understand, desire, and purchase them. Science will be a big driver of new products and services that will be available, and it will be up to marketers to craft messaging that translates the science into consumer benefits.

In my humble opinion, it's not always the early companies that make new technologies popular. It's the companies that find the best way to adapt these technologies to consumers' needs that succeed at commercializing technology. And this is where the midsize companies can compete.

> **For CEOs:** Looking for a product category that needs more marketing to succeed? Look no further than the cannabis market. After decades of cannabis use being stigmatized, it's going to take a lot of marketing to change attitudes and, in turn, regulations about CBD gummies for the general population.

Look at some of the new ideas that are already emerging as new product categories. Take changes in financial options, like cryptocurrencies and NFTs. Now *there's* a category that needs a little messaging lift. A young friend of mine moved to San Francisco right out of college and uses dating apps to meet new people. She told me that she has had a continual string of "tech bros" who insist on spending at least twenty minutes of the date explaining cryptocurrencies to her, even if she has never asked about them.

But NFTs are already finding their way into brand campaigns and are being featured in the metaverse. While this early work is being funded by larger brands, these digital tools will become more commonplace for marketing teams. Personally, I am all for the metaverse, as I can have an eternally smoking-hot physique without ever working out. I mean, talk about a value proposition!

The changes in the automotive industry, from EVs to self-driving vehicles, are also astounding to contemplate. Think about the communications strategy that will be necessary to bring consumers along with these bold technology conversions. Especially since the traditional giants in this category are the major advertisers across all channels that have been selling the internal combustion engine "the American way" to the population for years. The new generation of marketers will need to narrate a different way forward.

Even categories that are near and dear to consumers, such as food and health care, are going to be reengineered. We are seeing the early success of more earth-friendly food options like plant-based "meat." We are also seeing the rise of vertical farming in urban and suburban areas, so transportation costs are removed from the equation of feeding people in densely populated areas. Marketers will play a key role in moving these food solutions from the "tree huggers" to the mainstream.

Some naysayers claim these are food fads versus real trends, but it's hard to argue with the numbers. According to a new report by Grand View Research, the global plant-based meat market size is projected to reach $24.8 billion by 2030. The market is expected to expand at a compound annual growth rate (CAGR) of 19.3% from 2022 to 2030. The growing adoption of a vegan lifestyle among health-conscious consumers in traditionally meat-eating developed economies is driving the change. Some of the big players in this area—Beyond Meat, Impossible Foods, and Maple Leaf Foods—are influencing this trend through B2B and B2C marketing. These companies are collaborating with fast-food joints and restaurant chains to promote the adoption of their products. And now, plant-based meat is predominantly consumed in the hotels/restaurants/cafés (HORECA) sector. This combination of midsize companies and powerhouse brands can help us shift the planet to a more sustainable way of enjoying a burger or breakfast sandwich.[1]

Perhaps health care will have the biggest changes and challenges for marketers. Very few Americans would give the health care system good marks. From access and insurance to quality of care and eroding trust, it is a category ready for disruption and reinvention. Already we see millennials and Gen Zers doing their own research online about medical conditions, and they are less likely to take the advice of their doctor—*if* they have one. Even my Gen Z daughter said that while waiting to get an appointment, she found someone on Reddit who had a face rash similar to hers. When the doctor gave her conflicting advice, she admitted to being confused about whom to trust.

The new healthcare options will require marketing to develop trust and introduce new solutions as people have to become their own health advocates. Telemedicine, which exploded in popularity during the pandemic, is another example of how consumers are taking charge of their own care. Healthcare apps are now becoming mainstream, allowing people to speak to a

---

[1] https://www.grandviewresearch.com/industry-analysis/plant-based-meat-market?utm_source=prnewswire&utm_medium=referral&utm_campaign=cmfe_1-february-22&utm_term=plant-based_meat_market&utm_content=rd

doctor or even get a prescription. Even people who have a regular doctor may sidestep the wait for an appointment and opt for an app such as GoodRx, HeyDoctor, or one of the many others. Marketers will have to introduce these solutions to the mass market who have not yet made this behavioral leap.

In a recent conversation I had with a marketing consultant in the health care industry, he described how access to health care, especially mental health care, has become a critical issue in the US. He shared that over 18% of Americans have some mental health concern—and only half get treatment.

The other surprising stat he shared is that 30 to 40 percent of mental health practitioners' time is spent on things other than treating patients. Clearly, there is an opportunity in the future to bring more efficiency and efficacy to the industry. Smaller practices could benefit from electronic medical systems technology, telemedicine technology and training, digital marketing expertise, and combined negotiating leverage with insurance providers. This would give them more freedom to do what they set out to do: spend time with patients.

Asking private practices to join a holding company is a paradigm shift for professionals who have spent years building their businesses. It is a B2B marketing communications effort to explain how a business owner could benefit from that strategy. The B2C value proposition would be clear: better access to more mental health care providers through either in-person or telemedicine with lower costs and more providers accepting insurance plans.

My consultant friend went on to explain that health care is very local and very fragmented. The situation with mental health care providers is not dissimilar from the situation with dental practices, eye doctors, etc. As larger holding companies step in to help small providers with their back-of-the-house administration, we may see a total shift in the healthcare land-scape—hopefully, one that includes more accessible and afford-able care for the consumers. The midsize marketer's challenge of the future? Help change consumer behavior and business mod-els as we shift basic practices such as how we go to the doctor.

So many exciting health technologies are on the horizon and should be ready to scale in the future with the help of messaging and marketing. I personally geek out when learn-ing about genomes and DNA-specific personalized health care. We are seeing more DNA-specific treatment in advanced cancer treatments and in the area of mental health. Midsize company Genomind is a great example of a pioneering company in this space. Genomind first came to market with a product to use teens' DNA to help doctors prescribe the medicine most likely to work for their young mental health patients. Treatments that are personalized to a teen's molecular makeup have a better pos-sibility of producing positive outcomes when treating them for mental illness. While Genomind started with a vision to bring genetic insights to mental health treatment, they have expanded and transformed into a revolutionary precision health platform. It will be up to the marketers to bring terms such as *pharmaco-genetic testing* to the mainstream as personalized health care becomes more accessible.

There is an inexhaustible list of innovations percolating in our midst. And they will all need marketing to bring them to life for the people who will benefit from them. I'm sure you can share in my optimistic point of view that the future for midsize marketers is bright. It is a changing environment for consumers as we (the all-humankind "we") pivot to counteract climate change, use technology to advance health and wellness, and explore new ways of enjoying the human experience. Every big idea, scientific breakthrough, and technology game changer needs to be communicated to the people it will impact. And that's where the marketers come in.

To the next generation, the CMOs, and the CEOs of the companies that will bring about these changes, find the size of the organization that will fit your personal style and aligns with the changes you want to champion in your career.

THE MAGIC OF MIDSIZE

n *The Infinite Game*, Simon Sinek states, "We can't choose the game. We can't choose the rules. We can only choose how we play."

It is in that spirit that I assembled this book. For those who are passionate about marketing and are looking to find their career fit in the workplace, I hope these chapters offer a useful perspective. We are all looking for the best way to play the game, so we do what we love in an environment where we can thrive.

I focus on midsize organizations because company size, in my work experience, has shown up as a real differentiator in organizational behavior and culture. I have categorically found that the smaller organizations gave me a chance to grow. I was able to try new skills, play a little over my head until I figured it out, and use management skills, not just marketing skills.

It was gratifying to hear other professionals' points of view on the midsize vibe as I interviewed others for this book. CEOs, especially those of private equity portfolio companies, have talked to me about how vital a smart, efficient marketing team is to them while trying to create growth. Some knew exactly what they were looking for in a CMO and in a team. Others asked for the first copy of this book. (Why do CEOs always want things for free?)

In talking to CMOs, I asked broad questions about their experiences in larger companies versus midsize, and the feedback I received was as individual as the person. Some had always been with a large-cap industry giant, and others would weigh in that they loved their cool midsize tech company until it became huge and impersonal, and the original team members all left.

What many are looking for, especially the next generation, is a culture that fits their personal style. For me, I consistently found better cultures that suited my ambitions at midsize companies. I'm not saying the smaller orgs have a lock on team and camaraderie. Large companies that focus on culture or are centered around a purpose can also be appealing. Take Patagonia, for example. Selling all those puffy vests has put them into the big leagues, but their mission is, "We're in business to save our home planet." That is a purpose that could get you out of bed every morning.

Amy Parker has been a successful CMO at both large and midsize retail companies. When I asked Amy about her take on working midsize versus corporate, she told me about one of her favorite experiences at a midsize company called Pet Supplies Plus.

"As you can guess by the name, Pet Supplies Plus is a mid-size chain of owned and franchised pet supply stores. When we embarked on a corporate brand refresh, the process was completely grassroots. It involved everyone from store personnel and franchisees to warehouse and office staff. When all the input was compiled, a clear theme emerged: it's all about pet lovers. And that translated into our brand statement: 'Always trust a pet lover.'

"Then we all lived the brand. HR started incorporating questions about pet ownership and pet affinity into hiring conversations. They also added benefits that helped employees who were adopting a pet have adequate time with them in those early days. Internally, we initiated Fur-i-Days Fridays, a day when people could bring their pets into the office. It changed the whole tenor of the office environment and allowed people to create relationships. Everyone saw one another as a pet lover, and conversations often opened with questions about Tripod, the three-legged cat, or the new doggie adoption. The merchandising group had a lizard, the real estate team had a rabbit, and even the CEO had his cockatiel and dog.

"I still think back on how that corporate brand focus opened up trust with one another across every department—and made a productive culture for pet lovers."

Culture is how the company runs and how the people pull together (or do not) for the common purpose. I poked a little fun at internal theater and some of the bureaucracy of larger companies because those are cultural elements I could do without. At the same time, I've had the pleasure of being in cultures where people banded together, had a little fun, worked a lot of hours, and accomplished goals as a team. When I interviewed professionals about where they most enjoyed working, all of them cited places with great people or a great culture. More than one interviewee used the phrase, "It was a place where I could be my authentic self." Not one of them mentioned salary as making a place "the best."

As I am writing this, there is a revolution taking place in the workforce; more people are working from home and collaborating virtually. It will be interesting to see if this shift changes the importance of organization size. I am also fascinated to see how organizations that establish predominantly or wholly work-from-home staff create culture and community. Midsize companies will need to find ways to make their companies and offices places that attract talent.

Whether you are looking for the next step to take in your marketing career, looking to crush it on a midsize marketing team, or looking to hire the right mix of marketing players to grow your midsize company, I hope that you have found some useful strategies here to ensure your success. If you have found this book to be helpful or amusing, or if you wondered whether or not I was talking about you, reach out and let me know, and perhaps share *Midsize* with a friend.